ICE-SKATING—A HISTORY

A

ICE-SKATING

A HISTORY

BY NIGEL BROWN

NICHOLAS KAYE

LONDON

First published by
NICHOLAS KAYE LIMITED
194-200 Bishopsgate, London, EC2
1959

Printed in England by
ADLARD AND SON LIMITED
LONDON AND DORKING

TO MY WIFE,
ALBA ROVIDA,
AS A TRIBUTE TO HER LOVE OF,
AND ARTISTRY IN, THE
ART OF SKATING,
THIS HISTORY IS DEDICATED

ACKNOWLEDGMENTS

Photographs are gratefully acknowledged to Dick Button; Mrs Theresa Weld Blanchard; T. D. Richardson; Longmans, Green and Co.; G. Bell and Sons; Watts and Co., reproduced from *The Poetry of Skating* by Edgar Syers; John Wilson, Marsden Bros and Co.; Central Press Photos; P. A. Reuter Photos; Twentieth Century-Fox Film Co.; Rimis, London; Photo Peter Kaufman; Moss Photo Service Inc., New York; J. M. Schlemmer, Photo; 60 *Jahre Sportplatz Engelmann*, Wien 1932; Photo Baatard Villars; Photo Karl Schleich, Vienna; ATB Bilderdienst, Zürich; Photopress, Zürich; Photo Gehri, Davos; Davos Kurverein; Photo Hughes, Megeve.

The author has made every attempt to establish the ownership of each photograph used, but in those cases where this has not been possible, he trusts this general acknowledgment will be accepted.

The author also wishes to thank Dr J. Koch and Herr G. Häsler, President and Hon. Secretary of the International Skating Union, who have been very helpful on several occasions.

CONTENTS

PART ONE

EARLY TIMES

PART TWO

THE PIONEER STAGE

7

PART THREE

THE HEROIC ERA

PAGE

CONTENTS

LIST OF ILLUSTRATIONS

FOREWORD

The aim of this book is to portray the development of ice-skating from its beginnings as a means of transport among primitive man to its present-day status as an art. Therefore the story of skating and not the exploits of skaters is the main theme. Where skaters are mentioned by name, it is because they have had a definite bearing upon the evolution of skating, whether regarded as an art or a sport.

Lausanne   NIGEL BROWN
October, 1958

PART ONE
EARLY TIMES

CHAPTER 1

ICE-SKATING may be divided into three distinctive parts: speed-skating, ice hockey, and figure-skating, more properly termed 'artistic skating'. This last branch comprises figure-skating, free skating, pair-skating and dancing on ice.

Speed-skating was the first to develop as a sport and, apart from improvements in style and equipment, does not differ much in its general aspect now from its early days.

On the other hand ice hockey and artistic skating have been revolutionized since their first appearance. The first is now a game of great skill and excitement, the second has come to align itself with the older arts of dancing and ballet.

It is with this aesthetic branch of ice-skating that this survey is concerned, and only when the other two forms have some bearing or influence upon figure-skating will they be touched on.

The First Skates
Early Scandinavian literature is full of allusions to skating, and this evidence would date the introduction of ice-skating at about AD 200. Mention is made of an iron skate being used, which would correspond to historical fact as this metal then first came into general use throughout the North.

But the discovery during the nineteenth century of ancient bone skates in Germany, Sweden, Switzerland, the Danube Valley and in England suggests that ice-skating may be much older than 1,700 years.

Sagas of Scandinavia also mention bone skates and it is this particular reference which undoubtedly suggests a far earlier existence. As the blade of the iron skate of AD 200 is believed to have been held in the form of a wooden shoe, this brings a further element, wood, into the early history of the skate. It suggests a wooden, a bone and an iron 'age' of skating.

It is not improbable that the skate first appeared in the late neolithic period. The lake-dweller of those times would quite likely use his rude dug-out boat as a form of sledge over the frozen water. When migrating with his family and possessions he might find his route blocked by snow or would be suddenly taken by surprise in a heavy snow-storm; or, when he wanted to move his snow-bound habitation to warmer and more hospitable regions, snow would force him to try and ease his transport problems to avoid sinking and being bogged.

The idea of attaching a flat piece of wood to each foot, large enough to keep his weight from sinking into the snow, would come naturally to him in attempting to solve the problem of travelling over the frozen surface. Thus the snow-shoe would be invented. With it man was able to hunt for his food even in deep snow, descend and climb, and he could slide sitting on a plank of wood.

But this means of travel would be limited to his own person. Whether he had his dug-out with him or not he would find it difficult to move his goods over heavily frozen surfaces with ease.

Therefore in order to reduce friction in sliding his rude vehicle over the frozen wastes, he would naturally think first of the snow-shoe, and so placing planks of wood under his baggage he would find it possible to glide over the snow quite easily. This primitive sleigh set upon wooden runners could well be the first vehicle that existed on earth.

The Bone Skate

Early man would also discover that bone runners were better than wood for gliding over the ice. This material would be just as easy to obtain as wood for people who lived so largely on the products of the chase. There would always be at their disposal a surplus of bones, and some of these, fashioned as primitive skates, are now in a number of European museums.

To establish the approximate date of the first use of bone

1. A SPLIT JUMP BY DICK BUTTON. This dynamic American
World Champion changed the face of skating after World
War II, by introducing high-powered athletic feats

2. (above) ST LIEDWI'S ACCIDENT IN 1396. The Patron Saint of skaters. (From a wood engraving of 1498 in Brugman's *Vita Lijdwine*, the earliest skating print known)

3. (below) AN EARLY DUTCH SKATING SCENE, 1570

4. (above) FAIR ON THE FROZEN THAMES, 1683. This remarkable frost lasted from the beginning of December until February of the following year

5. (below) THE SKATE MAKER, 1694. (From the painting by Jan Luikjen)

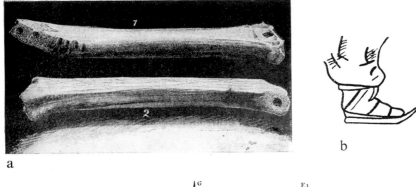

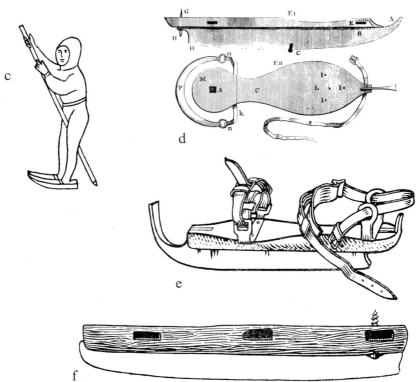

6. THE DEVELOPMENT OF THE SKATE.
From earliest times to the nineteenth century

a. Bone runners discovered in London Wall in the last century
b. Iron-bladed skate in use in the Netherlands in 1498
c. Iron-tipped staff to help the skater to steer and brake, still used in the middle of the sixteenth century
d. Bladed skate of 1772 (Robert Jones's period)
e. German skate of 1825 of Dutch origin, showing an improved fastening, with the toe-strap advanced to the ball of the foot
f. English skate of 1850, with the blade prolonged to the end of the heel

skates is not possible, but the area in which they were in use can be accurately defined, including Denmark, Holland, Northern Germany, Bavaria, Bohemia, Switzerland, Sweden, Norway and England.

Ever since the finding of such bones in the nineteenth century, there has been considerable controversy as to just how these primitive skates were used.

The bones were the metacarpal bones of horses, oxen, deer and sheep, and varied in length from eleven to twelve inches. At one end, the articulating joints have been shaved crudely off, and made to taper away sharply to a point forming the 'prow' of the skate, through which a hole has been drilled. The other end is roughly trimmed square and a hole drilled at the back running right through the bone stem. Through these holes were slipped leather thongs to attach the skate to the foot. The anterior surface is ground flat. Careful study of this polished part of the bone reveals it to be the result of deliberate grinding, and not the consequence of continual friction with the ice.

Such a bone may first have been used as a sledge-runner, and as late as 1882 sledges with similar bone runners were used by fowlers in the Fen district of England. These sledges or 'stalking-horses' as they were termed, were used by the hunter to get within shooting distance of wild ducks swimming in some still unfrozen water without disturbing them. The hunter lay prone upon the sledge with a screen of reeds in front. The butt of his long duck-gun was in position at the shoulder, with its muzzle just protruding through the mask of reeds, leaving both his hands free to hold two short sticks shod with iron spikes which he required to push and propel the sledge over the ice.

Children in North-east Prussia used to play on a sled called a *piekschlitten* in the middle of the nineteenth century. It was a crude contraption—a primitive sleigh, just a board nailed across some bones, and the children pushed themselves along similarly.

This method of propulsion was probably adopted by early man, for the lower ends of horses' shin-bones sharpened to a point are often found alongside the discoveries of bone skates.

17

Fitzstephen's chronicle of the twelfth century describes how bones tied to the feet were used to slide on, with a small staff or stick to aid propulsion.

These sticks were necessary, as it appears to be impossible to get an edge, that is, to 'strike' with a bone implement which would not cut into and grip the ice. Movement therefore would seem only to be obtainable by shoving with a staff in the manner of a modern punting pole to make a strike, push and steer.

A very interesting experiment was carried out by Mr G. Herbert Fowler, a great skating enthusiast and distinguished member of the Skating Club and the National Skating Association during the 1890s, who made a pair of bone skates copied from those found in 1869 and exhibited in the Guildhall Museum, London, and actually skated on them. Although he found that a stroke could not be taken off the side of the skate, it could be made off the toe, which was sufficiently strong to bite the hard ice of the National Skating Palace, and would of course bite and grip more readily the softer outdoor ice. Mr Fowler's experiment is significant in that it demonstrates the possibility of these primitive bone runners having been used centuries ago as skates proper.

An ancient bone fashioned as a skate with three holes drilled across it is in the Dutch museum at Groningen. These extra holes were undoubtedly for additional leather thongs which were used to fasten the skate more solidly to the foot, in the manner of Dutch skates of the last century. This refinement was a logical step, for by having the feet more securely held to the skates when striking off, the pointed pole became less of a necessity, allowing the bone skate to be used, and the hands remained free.

Mr Fowler's successful experiment tends to endorse this assumption. But until a less slippery substance was found than bone, no further progress was possible.

The First Iron Skate
There is not sufficient evidence to distinguish whether the skate itself or the pointed staff was the first to be shod with iron. It is

very probable that both benefited from this metal soon after its discovery.

The first iron skate would not be bladed but rather a strip fixed to a wooden block the length of a normal adult foot and would be shaped like a boat with a pointed prow that turned upward. Through two or more slits in the wood, leather thongs would be threaded to attach the whole to the foot in a similar manner to the earlier bone skate. At first the sole of the foot would be strapped to the wood, but later this was probably shaped in the fashion of a clog, into which the foot was slipped. This shoe form would hold the foot more firmly and with the new medium of iron would make it possible to give a powerful stroke.

This early iron skate resembles in some degree the modern snow-skate of Scandinavia. In the wilder parts of Norway, Sweden and Hungary, such skates were used for travelling over rough ice and hardened snow tracks during the latter part of the nineteenth century. After deep frost had followed a heavy thaw and made the surface of the snow impracticable for skiing, the only means of communication between one village and another was by this method. These skates are made of a wooden block, to the running surface of which is clamped a long strip of iron, twenty-four inches in length, two-fifths of an inch broad and an eighth of an inch thick. The edge of the iron strip is sharp enough to grip and allow a strong stroke. A pole is used, not in the primitive manner of pushing, but for steering and braking, while it is possible to keep up a good speed over frozen roads and beaten snow tracks.

The Norwegian Axel Paulsen, a brilliant exponent of skating skill in the 1880s improved this snow-skate considerably and traversed many districts of Southern Norway on snow-skates of his own design. These journeys of Axel Paulsen emphasize the possibilities and importance of the skate in the snow-bound countries of the North.

CHAPTER 2

Origin and Evolution of the Word 'Skate'

THE origin of the word cannot exactly be traced, but the Low German word *schake* meaning a shank- or leg-bone is indeed no coincidence, for we have already noted that the oldest skates recorded were made from the shank-bones of various animals. It is also interesting to note that the similar word *schenkel* meaning shank is used in Holland for the iron blade of the modern Dutch skate.

The modern French word *échasse* meaning a stilt is derived from a very old north-eastern French term *escache* which in turn is related to the much older Low German *schake* mentioned above.

A number of other words referring to a skate, such as *scacia* in Latin, *schaats* in Dutch, *skoite* in modern Danish and Norwegian, and *sketcher* in Scots originally implied a device for raising the wearer off the ground such as a stilt. Later the same words were also used to signify heavy wooden shoes or clogs that came into use.

The modern word 'skate' is no doubt derived from an earlier English word *scatch*, and by its root as well as its pronunciation suggests a close relationship to the old Picardy word already quoted, *escache*.

The modern Dutch word for skate, *schaats*, appears also to be similarly related to this early north-eastern French word, and it is more than probable that the English *scatch* is a deformation of the Dutch. Historical fact adds emphasis to such a theory, for it corresponds to the bringing to England of the modern art of skating on iron skates by the Stuarts when they returned from their exile in Holland at the end of the Commonwealth.

It is also feasible that the Anglo-Saxon word *scitan*, meaning 'to throw out'—the necessary action of the limbs in using skates—had also its role to play in the evolution of the modern word 'skate.'

The numerous terms in various languages that first designated a clog, a stilt or some device for raising the wearer off the ground and later were used in direct reference to a skate, appear to be of comparative antiquity; but the Low German word *schake* first mentioned, definitely appears much older in its connection with skating, in as much as it directly designates by its meaning the instrument, a shank-bone, that was first used as a primitive skate.

The Scandinavian Sagas

The earliest references to skating are to be found in the Scandinavian Sagas.

Owing to the rather liberal translation certain runic scholars have made of these works, some confusion has arisen where reference is made to gliding over the snow and ice, as to whether it is on skates or skis.

It is more than probable that these two means of locomotion developed at the same time, for both are obviously derived from the first sledge-runner or snow-shoe.

An early translation from the *Younger Edda*, a collection of Icelandic literature, reads:

'Uller, god of winter, runs on bones of animals over the ice.' A later and more correct version is, 'Uller is so good an archer, and so fast on his ski, that no one can contend with him.'

The main error has occurred in taking the word *skid*, meaning a ski or snow-runner, for a skate. But nevertheless it is not certain, even then, that a snow-skate is not meant.

There is evidence, however, that a wooden form of skate existed long before the Christian era. The curved toes of the ski or skate gave rise to the legend that the god was wafted over hill and dale on real ships—ships that sailed over the frozen waters.

However there is a passage in *Saxo Grammaticus*, relating that 'Oller was such a cunning wizard that he used a certain bone, which he had marked with awful spells, wherewith to

21

cross the sea, instead of a vessel, and that by this bone he passed over the waters that barred his way, as quickly as by rowing.'

In Bishop Percy's translation of runic poetry there is the passage where a northern hero, wishing to show his proficiency in many exercises claims:

'I am master of nine accomplishments—I play well at chess; I know how to engrave runic letters; I am apt at my book, and know how to handle the tools of the smith; I traverse the snow on skates of wood; I excel in shooting with the bow and in managing the oar; I sing to the harp and compose verses'.

As regards the allusion to traversing snow on skates of wood, it is debatable whether it was performed on skis or on snow-skates in the manner of Axel Paulsen.

In the same collection, in the poem called his *Complaint*, Harold, the hero recites:

'I know how to perform eight exercises—I fight with courage; I keep a firm seat on horseback; I am skilled in swimming; I glide along the ice on skates; I excel in darting the lance; I am dexterous at the oar; and yet a Russian maid disdains me.'

While allowing for liberal translation and the difficulty in interpreting clearly the difference between skiing and skating over snow and ice, because of the lack of definite data about the actual means used for this purpose, there is nevertheless no doubt that skating as a means of locomotion was considered a most notable accomplishment in the North.

The Earliest Literary and Pictorial Records

The first concrete evidence of actual skating on ice is found in a passage of Fitzstephen's *Description of the most noble City of London*, which was written in Latin and published in 1180. This twelfth-century chronicler was a clerk to the Archbishop Thomas-à-Becket. His work was translated by Stow, the sixteenth-century London chronicler.

The passage quoted so many times must of necessity be

repeated here, for it is a landmark in the story of skating:

'When the great fenne or Moore (which watereth the walles of the citie on the North side) is frozen, many young men play upon the yce, some stryding as wide as they may, doe slide swiftly . . . some tye bones to their feete, and under their heeles, and shoving themselves by a little picked staffe, doe slide as swiftly as a birde flyeth in the aire, or an arrow out of a crossbow. Sometime two runne together with poles, and hitting one the other, eyther one or both doe fall, not without hurt; some break their armes, some their legs, but youth desirous of glorie, in this sort exerciseth it selfe against the time of warre.

. . . Thus ferre FitzStephen of sports.'

In this description of Londoners at play it will be seen that such skating was a form of sliding only. A pointed staff or pole was essential to give the push necessary to obtain momentum. This suggests that in England at any rate, iron skates had not yet made their appearance in the reign of Henry II.

One very interesting fact that emerges from the last phrase in the passage is the allusion to playing a sort of game, running together with poles and striking at one another in an attempt to knock each other off balance. It was no doubt inspired by the tournaments of the period, and although practised in an exaggerated, brutal manner, it does emphasize the extra pleasure obtainable on the ice by collective, as well as individual sliding.

The earliest known pictorial record of skating was printed in Holland in 1498, and portrays the unfortunate accident that befell the sixteen-years-old Liedwi (who was born in 1380) when she was knocked down on the ice by one of her girl companions and broke a rib. Never completely recovering from this mishap, she spent the rest of her life in contemplation in a religious house and is considered the skaters' patron saint.

This old woodcut is astonishingly rich and shows a number of skating details.

The skate seen on Liedwi's foot is bladed, which means it was made of iron. The man in the background, coming over to her

23

assistance, is gliding over the ice, throwing out his legs in the manner of a modern skater, which indicates that he is able to make a strike off an edged blade. This suggests that skating proper by both young girls and men was already in vogue in Holland in the fourteenth century. It is therefore very likely that a bladed skate existed well before this date.

Long before the twelfth century, it may well be that sliding on bone runners was introduced into England with other customs during the conquests of the Danes and later by the Normans in 1066. Similarly, Holland early developed skating, but primarily out of necessity and utility as a means of locomotion over the frozen canals.

In Scandinavia where sliding over snow (skiing) and sliding over ice (skating) were both practicable, both forms no doubt existed and developed at the same time, but in the Low Countries and England the correct reference would nearly always be to skating and not to skiing.

CHAPTER 3

The Dutch Roll

ALTHOUGH skating—sliding over ice—was practised in a certain measure during the Middle Ages in various parts of Scandinavia, it was without doubt in the Netherlands that it was practised most.

The majority of the numberless lakes and rivers in Norway, Sweden and Finland that froze for a greater part of the winter were covered with blankets of heavy deep snow. This would restrict skating to the few clear stretches of rivers and lakes that escaped the severe snow-falls.

In the Netherlands the conditions were quite different. The country was threaded with canals, forming the main arteries of communication between one town and another, and in winter these long stretches of artificial rivers were frozen, but not often covered by deep snow. Through the medium of skates, they became the best and fastest means of communication between the towns and villages. In deep winter they were often the only means of reaching a place.

It cannot be exactly stated just when iron was used as a blade for a skate, but what can be safely assumed is that such an instrument was first developed in the Netherlands. The use of a metal blade allowed the wearer to get a grip upon the ice, which meant he was no longer dependent upon the staff or long pole for propulsion.

This was an enormous step forward in the art of skating, and it now remained to find a method of using these instruments in a comfortable manner, so that the wearer could glide over the ice as naturally and easily as he could walk or run.

The early user of iron skates, freed from the limitation of being dependent upon a pole for pushing, would no doubt attempt to gain momentum by running, and then allowing the

25

skates to slide over the ice until all impetus was lost, and this process would be repeated. It was quicker than walking over the ice, but if exhilarating and enjoyable, it was not very practical. It is of course a natural approach, for even beginners today, who have not been shown the first steps in skating, in spite of seeing the simple actions of skaters around them, run and slide in this primitive manner. The early skater would not be long content with this unsatisfactory manner of sliding over the ice, and it was probably quite early after the use of iron blades that he discovered the 'Dutch roll', the natural method for skating, made possible by the two-edged blade of iron, a skate having an 'outside' and an 'inside' edge.

By the latter part of the sixteenth century, the iron skate and the ability to control and use it correctly had reached a certain degree of perfection.

In 1572 the Dutch patriot fleet was frozen in the waters of the Y, and Don Frederick, son of the notorious Alva, despatched a body of picked men to cross the vast sheet of ice and capture the vessels. They were stopped however before a trench of water the Dutch had cut round their fleet. The Spaniards were forced to retreat, and then a body of Dutch musketeers advanced on skates and completely routed them, leaving several hundred dead upon the ice.

There has been much controversy about this interesting episode. Some claim that it was not upon skates that the valiant Dutchmen routed the Spanish arquebusiers, but upon a form of clog, with spiked nails to grip the ice. These undoubtedly formed part of their winter equipment. Such shoes would be absolutely necessary to a fighting man who had to traverse vast stretches of frozen ice for at least a quarter of the year.

But this form of shoe existed several centuries before and was in common use in various parts of Europe. There is every reason therefore to assume that the Spanish had knowledge of this clog and used it in a very limited way for small detachments of their armies doing service in the Netherlands during the winter.

An experienced soldier like Don Frederick would not send

his troops to attack the Dutch ships over so difficult and slippery a terrain as the ice presented, without having some means to give his soldiers a fairly solid foothold, to keep them from slithering about like drunkards.

Assuming that the attack was planned as a surprise, and that Frederick expected to engage in battle only when he got aboard the ships, the initial part of the project would have to be carried out stealthily, and this would need footwear giving security and stability upon the ice. In fact the surprise of Alva after the battle is proof that it had not occurred to the Spanish command that such a combat was possible on the ice.

When the Spaniards discovered the deep moats around the fleet they retreated. The Dutch then coming out on skates would easily be able to cut off such a manoeuvre and to attack and slaughter the enemy.

The clogs worn by the Spaniards gave them a strong foothold, but their movements would have been restricted, whereas the Dutch on their skates possessed complete and easy mobility, being able to dash forward, retreat backwards and sideways, and to turn at will. They were just as much at ease as if they were on land, with the additional advantage of speed. Alva, impressed by this power of the Dutch on skates, immediately ordered 7,000 pairs of skates for his own troops. They were drilled regularly in this new exercise and the fact that after a year's training it was found they had not mastered the art, suggests that skates as well as spiked clogs were used in this battle, and were the main contribution to the Dutch victory.

Further evidence of skating in the Netherlands is found at the siege of Haarlem.

It was impossible for the Spaniards to starve out this Dutch town in the depth of winter, for so long as the Haarlem mere was frozen, they could not prevent men, women and even children skimming over the ice and bringing provisions and arms to the besieged. It was only when the frost broke up that the siege became effective and the town could be starved.

27

Skating as a Sport

As mentioned earlier in Fitzstephen's vivid description, the young people of London tried to race one another across the ice, pushing vigorously with their poles in an attempt to be the first at the other end. This would mean that sliding on ice was a sport since a competitive element was introduced. Nevertheless no really skilled form of sport or game in the true sense was possible, until a proper and efficient skate had been invented that could grip the ice, and a method found to use it efficiently.

The invention of the iron skate and the discovery of the Dutch roll immediately transformed sliding over ice into a science. The pushing pole had been discarded, and a natural way of moving over a frozen surface had been found.

Although it took a certain time and skill to acquire proficiency and ease in this new science, sliding over ice was now a performance of skill, it was skating. With the aid of iron keels attached to his feet, man became just as much at his ease on ice, as he was walking across a field or running along a road, and he could move at speed.

Swiftness is the thrill that skating first gives to the novice. It remains throughout the skater's career, for speed belongs to skating. Speed-skating, racing, would therefore appear to be of primary importance in the organized development of skating. Conclusive evidence of prints of the period show this form of ice-sport to be highly developed already in the sixteenth century in Holland where both men and women competed for honours before large crowds.

Skating was now an established sport.

Skating as a Pastime

There is no doubt that well before the middle of the seventeenth century ice-skating had become an important recreation in Holland. Several notable Dutch painters turned to the frozen ponds for inspiration. Life there was colourful and gay. It was practised by every class of society, from the simple peasant to the princes themselves.

28

It was especially amongst the nobility that skating found its true beginnings as a sport. Although the form in which it was practised in the early part of the seventeenth century was not yet really skating as such, it was an established pastime destined to develop rapidly into a science.

While speed would be the main preoccupation of the peasants hurrying to the market over the frozen canals to sell their wares, of the youths challenged to race their nearest companion, and of the soldier whose duty it was to move faster than the enemy, it would not have the same necessity or appeal to the nobleman. *Le grand siecle* had just begun. Refinement and grace were a nobleman's passport. Exaggerated speed on ice, and the manner of performing it would appear vulgar to him. To his refined tastes it was an exercise of no appeal.

The influence of elegance and good manners cannot be overestimated when following the early development of skating. It was this aristocratic interest which laid the foundation-stone of artistic skating.

Sliding over ice in an elegant fashion, listing over in a Dutch roll, gliding over the glistening surface balancing one foot high behind like a graceful dancer had an irresistible attraction.

Under the influence of princely company, skating unconsciously acquired the dignity of the courtly circles. Arms and legs were poised with deliberate elegance. Heads were held high—grace was a part of skating.

By the middle of the seventeenth century skating in Holland was a national pastime. In winter the frozen canals not only served as the best means of communication between one village and another, but were the scenes of popular race-meetings, and the settings of colourful merry-making.

The canals, like streets, were often transformed into town squares reminiscent of the gay and lighthearted piazzas of Southern Italy. Good thick ice in winter time in Holland heralded festival time.

Tents were erected along the shores, fires were lighted upon the ice, and ships, small canal barges with long skate-runners attached to their hulls, and sails flying, were used to transport the gentry to their rendezvous.

When the Stuarts were exiled in Holland during Cromwell's Protectorate, they learnt to skate and perform the Dutch roll. The Duke of Monmouth, son of Charles II, is recorded as having taught the English country dance to the ladies of the Dutch court, who in turn showed him how to execute the 'outside and inside edge'. He often accompanied the Princess of Orange who contributed to a valuable step in the evolution of skating. She discovered that a special costume was necessary for the sport, and although it was at the time when to show an ankle was to raise a blush, she had the courage and intelligence to abandon her lengthy, draping skirt and tuck her unusually short petticoats half-way up to the waist, in order to allow the essential freedom of action so necessary when skating.

It is significant to note that this neither raised a scandal nor shocked the courtly circles who appreciated that this was necessary if pleasure and grace were to be achieved. The ease and sureness with which the male skater could move because of his attire would be in striking contrast to the cumbersome long skirts of his female companion.

However the incident appears to have afforded a mixture of both wonder and mirth for those who witnessed the scene, for the French ambassador to the Netherlands made the following comment on it in a despatch to Louis XIV:

'Twas a very extraordinary thing to see the Princess of Orange clad in petticoats shorter than are generally worn by ladies so strictly decorous, these tucked up half-way to her waist, and with iron pattens on her feet learning to slide sometime poised on one leg sometime on another.'

The fact that so many eminent people witnessed this episode emphasizes that skating had become a fashionable pastime.

PART TWO
THE PIONEER STAGE

CHAPTER 4

The Introduction of Skating into England

ALTHOUGH a primitive form of sliding on shank-bones had existed in various parts of England for some considerable time, there is little doubt that real skating performed on iron-bladed skates was not practised here before the Restoration. Very definite evidence of this is given by Hexham, in his *English and Netherduytch Dictionarie* published in 1648 when he speaks of 'skates which they slide upon the Yce in Holland'. This would infer that the shank-bone such as had been used at various times in the Middle Ages in England was not then referred to as a skate, and no doubt was termed a 'Scatch, a Sketcher or even a simple Yce-bone'. As Hexham translates it, a 'skate' would refer to an iron-bladed shoe as used by Dutchmen for the purpose of sliding over the ice.

When the Stuarts returned to England they carried with them two amusing novelties, iron-bladed skates and the Dutch roll.

On 1st December 1662, Samuel Pepys witnessed an extraordinary sight upon the new canal in St James's Park.

He entered that day in his diary the following significant sentence:

'To my Lord Sandwich's, to Mr Moore and then over the Parke where first in my life, it being a great frost, did see people sliding with their skeetes, which is a very pretty art.'

There are three things which make this quotation significant. Firstly, the mention of 'people sliding with their skeetes' undoubtedly refers to some contraption that was attached to their feet. This is probably the first use of the word 'skate' in direct reference to sliding over ice in England, and therefore would be the first mention of blade-skating in that country.

Secondly, it is highly improbable that Pepys, who was always on the look-out for novelties, should not have seen iron skates before this date, had there been any in England, or that he would not have recorded it.

Thirdly, and most important of all, he uses the word 'art'. This would mean he was considerably impressed by their performance on the ice. They must have been capable of a certain control, together with graceful attitudes and elegance in movement. 'Art' used by Pepys suggests that a certain science was evident among these seventeenth-century skaters.

That it was a remarkable sight to behold at that time is confirmed by Evelyn who recorded on the same day that he saw 'the strange and wonderful dexterity of the sliders on the new Canal in St James's Park, performed before their Majesties by divers gentlemen and others with Scheets, after the manner of the Hollanders, with what swifnesse they passe, how sudainly they stop in full carriere upon the ice. . . I went home by water, but not without exceeding difficultie the Thames being frozen, great flakes of ice incompassing our boats'.

It is interesting to note that Evelyn used a different spelling for skate to Pepys, *scheets* resembling almost identically the modern Dutch word for skate, whereas Pepys' term is all but the equivalent of the English word used today.

Evelyn's term and reference to Hollanders suggests he gathered his information from some of the exponents on the spot and recorded exactly what he was told, which again shows that this science was not only new in England, but had been brought to the country by English exiles from the Netherlands.

A fortnight later Pepys gives further evidence of the important role played by Royalist exiles and even by the Royal family itself in introducing and popularizing skating in England.

The celebrated diarist accompanied the future James II to an ice-bound pond to see him skate. It showed Pepys' interest in the new science as well as the Duke's virtuosity as a skater.

The entry reads:

'15th December 1662. To the Duke and followed him into

the parke where, though the ice was broken and dangerous, yet he would go slide upon his scates, which I did not like, but he slides very well.'

The nervousness that Pepys showed for his Royal companion appeared only to be equalled by the Duke's daring and skill.

The year 1662 is a red-letter date in the story of skating. A new recreation was introduced into a country which was always quick and ready to seize and adopt a novelty in the sphere of exercise. There is no doubt that skating with iron-bladed skates began its conquering career among Englishmen from then on.

For twenty-one years later when the Thames froze hard from December until 5th February, many Englishmen and among them Samuel Pepys possessed a certain proficiency in the elegant and graceful movements of this new art.

The Great Frost of 1683 was the occasion of special festivities in London. A great fair was constructed on the frozen river and the sports of bull- and bear-baiting, and fox-hunting, as well as skating, took place on the ice. King Charles II with Queen Catherine arrived in a sledge drawn by a skater, and received guests on the ice-bound river, among them Nell Gwynn and Samuel Pepys.

Although many Londoners no doubt showed fair skill in skating it was Dutch sailors who fascinated the crowds by their tricks. Contemporary ballads describe vividly such scenes.

The Rotterdam Dutchman, with fleet-cutting scates,
To pleasure the crowd shows his tricks and his feats;
Who, like a rope dancer (for his sharp steels),
His brains and activity lies in his heels.

The Dutchman hers, in nimble-cutting scates,
To please the crowd do show their tricks and feats.

The Dutch that in great
Large shoals used to meet,
And clapt their crook'd scates on their foot,

Now no more dare appear
To make folken stare
While on the smooth surface they float.

These ballads show conclusively how much more advanced the Dutch skaters were than the English at that time. They also point out that skating was still a pastime. There was probably quite a large Dutch commercial fleet anchored at the mouth of the Thames, and their crews would not hesitate to seize such a wonderful chance to career up 'Old Man Thames' on skates, showing off their ability and skill to the amazed Londoners.

With nine weeks of hard frost the sight became an everyday affair and the idea of sliding over the ice with iron skates no longer was considered as something extraordinary, nor any more a novelty, but just another recreation that Londoners wanted themselves to perform, and they certainly did so.

The First Skating Club
There can be little doubt that the feats and exhibitions of the Dutch sailors at the Great Frost Fair on the Thames in 1683 did much to make skating more widely known to a larger public in England. There must have been many converts who seized every opportunity when winters were hard to exercise themselves in this new fascinating outdoor recreation. From 1683 it may well be said that skating had become a part of English sports and pastimes and it quickly developed into a fashionable one.

Skating as practised at the time of the Great Frost Fair was later termed 'plain skating', for it was limited to the Dutch roll, to the outside and inside edges. Of course a number of daring and imaginative skaters lifted their free leg high and stretched their body well forward resembling a modest form of modern spiral. Prints of that period illustrate isolated skaters in such positions. There were certainly other small divergencies from the fundamental Dutch rolls, but they were all nevertheless restricted to the outside and inside edges.

During the previous century considerable numbers of refugees, fleeing before the fury of the Duke of Alva, settled in the Eastern Counties of England. The Fen district of all places in Britain would be where ice was abundant during hard winters, yet there is no actual record of these immigrants having introduced skating into England.

Further, when in 1625 Charles I engaged the great Dutch engineer, Cornelius Vermuyden, to drain the Isle of Axholme and various parts of the Eastern Counties he appears to have employed French and Flemish workmen, who would have known of skating although they may not have practised it in England. That the word 'pattens', meaning a pair of skates, was used in the Fen district right up until nearly the end of the nineteenth century indicates very conclusively that skating was introduced by French and Flemish refugees.

The point, however, which is important is that the type of society which did bring it to this waterlogged area was that of workmen or artisans whose skating activities would be confined to its utility as a form of locomotion, and where pleasure and fun entered, to speed.

It was however as a recreation that there were opportunities for an imaginative mind to turn it into something more than just the Dutch roll. The control and use of the outside and inside edges remained its basis, but that did not give complete mastery of movement on the ice. Absolute control of certain difficulties of balance had yet to be obtained and so long as skating continued to be an amusing and fashionable pastime would remain undeveloped until some kind of organizing element was introduced.

Such an important step was made in Scotland sometime during the second half of the eighteenth century when the Edinburgh Skating Club, the first ice club in the world, began its activities.

There is some doubt as to the exact date when this distinguished club was founded. Tradition suggests that meetings of the club were suspended in 1642 'owing to the melancholy and disturbed state of the country'. However this date does not correspond with the introduction of ice-skating into England and there is no evidence of ice-skating as such having been introduced into Scotland earlier than into England.

It is very probable that 1742 is meant, for this date would have a logical significance in reference to skating in Great Britain. It would be some eighty-odd years after the return of the Stuarts and give ample time for the development of skating and it would be reasonable for a club to be founded well before this date.

The oldest minute-book in the club's possession is dated 1784. The first entry reads:

> '30th January 1784. At a meeting of the skating club . . . it was unanimously resolved to appoint Mr John Rae, Assistant Secretary to Mr William Anderson, on account of Mr Anderson's bad state of health.'

Obviously the club had been formed some years earlier. Further, a list of members, 'made up from memory by a quorum of the Society in January 1778' contains the names of four who passed the entrance test that year.

Two encyclopaedias published in Scotland in the first half of the nineteenth century place the date of the foundation of the Edinburgh Skating Club in the last half of the eighteenth century, though they differ as to the year.

It may well be that this eminent club began its career sometime between 1683 and 1742, and in the latter year temporarily suspended its activities.

That the club played an active and important part in the early development of figure-skating may be judged from the severity of the tests held for a skater who wished to become a member of the club.

Although there is no complete record of the test for admission to the club in 1784, it was very probably similar or even the same as that demanded in the early part of the nineteenth century.

Then, it was necessary to skate a complete circle on either

foot. This would more or less correspond to a modern figure eight although each circle was performed independently and not to a centre as today. It was also necessary to jump over first one, two, and then three hats that were placed on the ice.

The last would require a certain amount of ability from quite a few club skaters today, and it shows how high the standard was within the club at that early stage of development.

Although such a feat of jumping over three hats cannot be truly termed an athletic performance, it does possess the ingredients of daring and courage on a dangerous surface such as ice, and shows very early one direction in which skating was destined to turn.

The contribution of the Edinburgh Skating Club so early in the real story of figure-skating cannot be over-estimated. It was the first organizing body that disciplined and guided skating into the right channels and popularized its practice among a wider circle. It may be claimed that through it the tradition of British influence on this new sport was to play such an important role up to modern times.

The First Figure-skate

Although the Dutch gentry skated as a pastime or means of travel and no doubt society elsewhere followed, no attempts at that early period of skating history were made on the part of its exponents to explore scientifically further into its possibilities. It was in England that skating was first developed as a sport.

It had begun as a pleasant winter exercise and the English characteristic love of recreation favoured the development of skating. Once having found the delights and the skill necessary to skim over frozen ice, they would not be long in trying to turn the pastime into a game or sport.

There was also another fundamental motive that helped the development of skating in this direction. Unlike Holland where it was more a necessity for getting about in winter time, skating in England was a pastime and began and centred on frozen ponds, and the continual execution of the same inside and outside edges would certainly become monotonous for the more ambitious skater. New exercises would be attempted. Some would be successful, some not. The aspiring performer would discover that he was handicapped by his skates which would not be adaptable to such swift movements.

When skates were first made in England they would be modelled upon the Dutch pattern, long and low-pitched, suitable for travelling distances on the ice. The evolution of pond-skating with its demands for a skate that was suitable for quick turns and the performance of circles within a small radius, produced the first English figure-skate.

Within a century of the introduction of skating into England there were already several primitive types of figure-skate in use. The iron blade was short and circular, not more than two inches of its surface touching the ice at a time. This was in strong contrast to the completely flat surface of the Dutch skate. This circular form of the English skate would enable the skater to turn in small spaces and would also accelerate the motion. The smaller base also required more skill for its wearer to keep in balance. These improvements were revolutionary and opened up to skating wide possibilities for the improvisation of intriguing exercises.

When this curved blade first appeared cannot be stated with precision. It may have been invented logically, for a flat blade causes considerable friction upon the ice, and sooner or later an improved skate would be invented to remedy this. Yet it seems just as likely that the curved blade was invented outright to conform with the requirements of early pond-skating.

The direction skating took in England after it had taken root was towards elegance in movement and this would necessitate an improvement on the long, flat and broad Dutch skate. A further characteristic of this early English skate was its higher iron blade, for graceful movement was difficult with the low Dutch skate which hindered inclination of the body and an elegant stance particularly on a long roll, in fact, a long outside edge was not really a possibility on such a skate.

The Dutch only began to curve and shorten their skates after the first half of the eighteenth century, and taking into consideration how advanced skating was in England by that date, it can be assumed that the English figure-skate came first.

By 1770 grooved skates were in use, popularly known then as 'fluted skates', but oddly enough they were not received well by exponents of the art. The short high curved blade appears to have better suited the skating requirements of the time. The main problem then appears to have been in finding a secure method for fastening them to the foot. The simplest system was by passing a tape through the holes in the front of the skate, which was then tied across the toes, passed through the rings in the heel of the skate and brought back again to be lightly fastened by a knot over the instep. This was a very primitive form of attachment, and was probably the original fastening on the first figure-skate. After the skater had been on the ice for a very short time they would naturally become loose and need re-tightening. This sort of insecure fixture increased the dangers of falling and so a better fastening had to be found.

Screws were used to hold the stock, or wooden base upon which the iron blade was threaded, to the boot. Some of these stocks were made of brass, and some had separate stocks of iron for the heel and the sole of the boot, a forerunner of the modern figure-skate. The iron however was carried over the edges of the boot soles and turned up, to hold the boot more firmly.

These two latter methods were extremely advanced in conception, yet they were not considered then as the most efficient means of fastening the skate to the boot. It was found that when the boots were screwed to the stocks the skates had no proper play and the ankles ran the risk of being sprained by sudden jerks of the skates, especially when going over rough ice. Larger boots remedied this but at the same time gave *too much* play resulting in irregular and uneasy progression.

The most popular method at that time was by holding the skate to the boot with tightly fixed toe- and heel-straps, and long screws which went through the back of the skate stock and

41

projected deeply into the heel of the boot. (Examples on Plate 6).

This eighteenth-century figure-skate with its curved radius and short blade was the first real step towards the foundation of figure-skating as an art. Though a comparatively primitive instrument, it was the consequence of logical thought and served admirably as a tool for sliding over the ice, and with its invention a new branch of ice-skating came into being in opposition to the older speed-skating. With the figure-skate, artistic skating had found its place.

The First Skating Textbook

In 1772 Robert Jones, a lieutenant of Artillery, wrote in the English language the first treatise on ice-skating. It was a textbook of 10,000 words containing valuable information on how to perform the various figures then known in figure-skating. So advanced was this study, apart from his frequent allusions to others, that it emphasizes very clearly that he must have had many keen and competent forerunners.

It shows how quickly figure-skating had developed in England after its introduction, for already a number of basic figures and free movements had been discovered to supplement the Dutch roll and formed a small repertoire of exercises upon the ice. Well before the middle of the eighteenth century artistic skating was a winter diversion of some importance in England. At the time of the publication of Robert Jones's book, it was already classified as an 'art'.

One peculiar element however was striking. In spite of the example given by the Princess of Orange and other noble ladies a century earlier, figure-skating as practised in England during these pioneer stages was exclusively a male occupation. Jones laments this fact and sees no reason why the ladies should be excluded. He shows a shrewd understanding of the possibilities of skating when he says 'No motion can be more happily imagined for setting off an elegant figure to advantage, nor does the minuet itself afford half the opportunity of displaying a pretty foot'. He goes on to point out the social opportunities that skating offers and his explanation suggests the pleasure skating offers as a recreation when practised by both sexes. He merits quoting again if only to illustrate his complete comprehension of the many qualities skating offered! 'A lady may indulge herself here in a tête-à-tête with an acquaintance, without provoking the jealousy of her husband; and should she unfortunately make a slip [sic], it would at least not be attended with any prejudice to her reputation.'

Robert Jones's study is divided into two parts and devoted to detailed explanation of the various exercises forming figure-skating and useful advice on how to learn and perform them well. The first part deals with the fundamental principles called 'plain skating' and 'graceful rolling', and is made up of the inside edge, the outside edge, and a long curved line on the outside edge, called 'rolling', 'running' and 'stopping', and thus completes the basic groundwork.

The inside edge was the first exercise the beginner attempted mainly because it was the most natural. Even today it is a common sight to see those who have received no instruction whatsoever take a few running steps and then place themselves on the inside edge and circle round. In 1772 it was not considered a good exercise and in fact was rarely practised by advanced skaters.

It was occasionally used by them to relieve and rest the skater after he had been travelling some time on the outside edge. It was looked upon in the same light in Holland and used only for short intervals during journeys of forty or fifty miles in one day. Since skating in England as practised on the frozen ponds at that time was solely interested in easy movements and graceful attitudes, many skaters never attempted to learn the inside edge which neither gave real pleasure to the skater nor to the spectator. Nevertheless Jones advised strongly its practice mainly as a rest from other movements.

The outside edge was naturally the goal of all beginners, and often took three or four winters in learning it, taking into consideration that winters were often mild and a season contained very few skating days. This edge as utilized by beginners and inexperienced skaters was used for travelling or rather circling over the pond. The Dutch method of holding their hands in their pockets was imitated as it was considered the best manner of acquiring an easy-going position. The Dutch who often skated thirty or forty miles in one stretch attained a rhythmic ease of action in this attitude. After the initial stage of their journey when a sufficient speed had been worked up, an automatic and balanced rolling action on the outside edge to suit each individual skater was held, and with hands in pockets, gave the skater a pleasant feeling of effortless motion as he glided from side to side along the frozen canals.

Variations of the outside edge as used as the logical action for going forward were made, and 'rolling on the outside edge', as it was called, was a form of spiral with the body steeply inclined towards the outside.

This exercise could only be carried out by taking a number of running steps first, and running then appears to have been the essential qualification for the achievement of the most ambitious exercises in skating, but it apparently had its perils. A great number of skaters were afraid to run for fear of falling and those who could run were always in danger of colliding with a fellow skater. Collisions were frequent, and resulting accidents often serious. It was necessary to learn to brake suddenly.

The method usually practised at that time was neither a natural skating action nor a very certain manner of braking. The skater leant well back on his heels bringing his entire weight upon the back of his skates, while the toes pointed into the air. Stopping in this fashion was never instantaneous and Robert Jones hastens to correct this uncertain way of braking. He recommends turning the feet to right or left and pressing on the inside of the leading foot. This method was a great improvement and is almost a modern interpretation, which oddly enough is the exact opposite of the one inexperienced skaters use today, the weight being placed on the outside, as in a Christiania position of a skier.

There was also a jumping brake, coming down with the feet parallel, turning them as much as possible to the right or left. This was a hardy feat and only practised by the more proficient performer.

When a skater had mastered the inside, outside and long outside roll, could run and stop efficiently, he was a skater of a certain merit and ready to attempt the 'more masterly parts of this art', provided of course he was naturally very active and 'possessed of some genius' as Jones put it.

The author's final phrase that closes his 'plain-skating' chapter is significant, for he not only meant that the higher branch of artistic skating contained important technical difficulties to be surmounted, but needed above all an inspiration of movement, a natural talent of using the body gracefully, for advanced skating then was the beginning of modern free skating.

The conclusions obtained from Robert Jones's interesting remarks on this section of skating will be dealt with in the next chapter, and emphasize the importance and value of the first skating textbook.

CHAPTER 5

The Early Stages of an Art

THE second part of Robert Jones's book deals principally with free-skating figures, or rather free-skating movements. Although he does not designate them as such, the important fact that emerges is the natural direction skating unconsciously took in the pioneer stages. It has already been pointed out how speed is the heart of skating, and speed needs space for its production and also to display it in its proper light. The movements which developed quickly in the eighteenth century were all based on swiftness of movement, and all the exercises needed space to execute them correctly. And this combined with elegance and grace of execution gave such performance real beauty of action. This was free skating, the apex of skating skill. The proficient skaters of the eighteenth century possessed all this in various degrees of skill.

The repertoire of free-skating movements which existed in 1772, if combined together were sufficient to form a modest free-skating programme, though it is doubtful whether any masters of the day attempted this. The spiral, the inside circle, the outside circle, the Flying Mercury, the Fencing Position, the Serpentine Line, the outside backward roll were all performed independently.

The spiral was attempted after a run of about thirty yards when the skater leant strongly over on the outside edge, at the same time throwing his body well forward, and bending his tracing knee. Particular importance was laid on the position of the arms which in this case adopted an attitude similar to an archer's at the moment of drawing his bow. As the long curve gradually lost momentum the body was raised slowly to an upright position and the free leg lowered accordingly until both legs were finally brought together. This completed the spiral but

46

it did not terminate the figure. Finish then was as important as it is necessary today. A small roll, an outside edge on the other foot was made, with one hand laid upon the hip, and the other raised slowly in harmony with the skating movement, high above the head with the eyes fixed upon it.

Two outstanding points emerge from the eighteenth-century execution of this basic free movement. Beauty of position was of course essential, but the harmonious play of arms for complete interpretation of graceful movement was very necessary. The termination of a beautiful free-skating movement with elegance and meaning was important too. A proficient skater of the eighteenth century would not think of merely executing the difficult technical part of the figure and leaving it at that. Skaters in those early days possessed all the understanding essentially needed for the development of the art. Graceful action is a vital part of skating and was never sacrificed by the eighteenth-century exponent because of possible difficulty of execution.

The inside circle was strongly recommended then because it teaches how to turn out the toes and therefore helps in the learning of other positions such as the inside Spread Eagle.

The outside Spread Eagle offered many difficulties and was mastered only by a few. It was considered a dangerous figure and a straining one, though its mastery gave the performer such command of his skates that coming off-balance or falling seemed out of the question. The outside Spread Eagle was then the ultimate in a skater's repertoire.

The Serpentine Line was the changing of edge performed on one foot in as straight a line as possible and repeated several times.

Skating backwards was neither considered necessary nor pleasant. It was exercised more as a caprice than a real skating movement.

An exercise which has its place of honour in skating history is the Salutation. It was a picturesque movement performed by two skaters at once, and so the ancestor of combined-skating which

47

in the next century was to become so popular in England. Both performers had to be of similar calibre and masters of the inside circle and rolling.

The two skaters stand opposite each other about twenty feet apart. They both take a strong stroke on the right outside edge towards each other, and as they pass they join hands only for the moment while crossing, then quickly turning themselves on their right foot, they strike off on the inside circle to the left, drawing their right legs in a manner as if making a bow in a minuet. At the beginning of this second stroke the hat is doffed low and the courtesy completed, both turn round on the left leg, replacing their hats as the turn is made, and resume their original positions.

However the most outstanding figure described by Robert Jones is the outside forward three, known just previous to the publication of his book. He calls it the 'figure of a heart on one leg', and after the three turn was executed the motion was continued until the skater joined the line where he had begun the heart.

The figure was no doubt performed over a large surface and was therefore considered a free-skating movement. The outside forward eight was also described though not so christened.

The first treatise on figure-skating included a number of plates of skaters in gorgeous dress and adopting elegant attitudes that were inspired from the Greeks. The author concludes his work by mentioning that there are many other movements employed in skating which he has not described for they are neither graceful nor pleasing. This fact alone is interesting and significant. Skating in the eighteenth century in England had become a young art. It was developing fast, and from the rough-and-tumble slithering and sliding of the common people, skating was created.

Figure-skating Becomes Universal
The completely new conception of skating that was developed in England from the primitive Dutch roll in the eighteenth

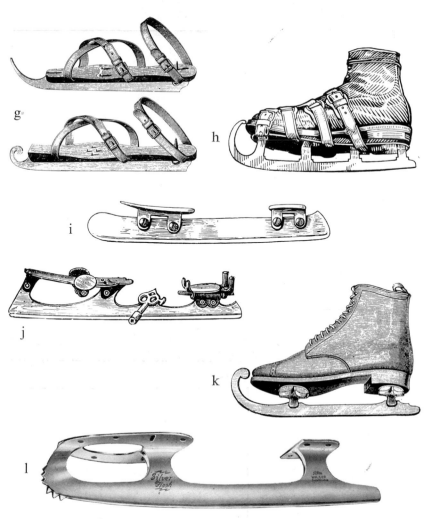

7. THE DEVELOPMENT OF THE SKATE. Modern times

g. English skates at the end of the nineteenth century, inspired by Dutch runners and used especially in the Fen district

h. American skate of 1860, with four straps and four skate-supports to make it rigid

i. Mount Charles figure-skate of 1905, the last souvenir of the 'English style'

j. 'Clamp on' figure-skate in vogue at the beginning of the twentieth century

k. Model for the 'international' style for nearly seventy years; this type of skate with boat-shaped prow and blade projection beyond the heel was used by Jackson Haines

l. The Silver Flash, one of the finest expressions of the modern figure-skate

8. (above) TWO SKATES SPECIALLY MADE FOR QUEEN VICTORIA AND PRINCE ALBERT. The makers were Marsden Brothers of Sheffield; this firm, now called John Wilson, Marsden Bros. and Co., have been skate makers since 1696

9. (right) GOETHE SKATING AT FRANK-FURT. End of the eighteenth century. (By Raab, after Von Kaulbach, 1862)

10. (left) JACKSON HAINES, 1865. Founder of the art of modern skating
11. (right) AN ENGLISH SKATER, 1780. (From the second printing of *Skating* by Robert Jones, 1797)

12. (left) LEOPOLD FREY, 1870. Viennese pupil of Haines, and winner of the first big international skating contest in 1882
13. (right) A *Gilet Rouge*, 1813. (From the first skating book in French, Garcin's *Le Vrai Patineur*)

14. FRANZ BELAZZI, 1867. Talented child skater from Vienna, and favourite pupil of Jackson Haines

15. (far right) AXEL PAULSEN, 1870. This skilful and inventive Norwegian skater did much to spread interest in skating in Europe and America

century soon had its happy echo in other countries in Europe.

It has already been stated that skating very probably filtered into France and Germany from Holland before the eighteenth century, but its practice was limited, in fact it can better be referred to as having been known in those countries and there it ended.

Several years after the publication of Robert Jones's book, skating in France was a fashionable recreation. It was as a pleasurable exercise that it established itself there, and its sudden appearance suggests that it came to France direct from England as a ready-made article. The court adopted it and gave it a place of honour in the *grandes fêtes* at Versailles. The sophisticated ladies of the court ventured on the ice in a sleigh draped in swansdown that slid slowly over the frozen surface of mirrored ice, while the nobles skated and courted the delicate figures that hid behind their snow-white masks. Marie Antoinette donned skates herself and showed the way for her sex to enjoy the delights of ice-skating. It is claimed she became one of the few outstanding lady skaters of that period.

It was, however, mainly a male occupation, and such was its success that it practically became necessary to add skating ability to a courtly education. One of the most celebrated fencers of the day, the Chevalier de Saint Georges who excelled in every outdoor sport, learnt to skate and became its most outstanding exponent in France at the time.

In Germany figure-skating appears to have taken root at a similar time as in France. By 1788 it was rapidly expanding, though somewhat behind England. Long curves and spirals on the outside edge were the main features then practised. Smaller figures and poses appear to have been treated contemptuously and termed 'artificialities'. However there must have been some inventive forces at work in search of new movements, for in that year the first important publication on skating was printed. It was in the form of a lecture delivered to a club of friends in Dessau, by G. U. S. Vieth, an enthusiastic skater who later played a considerable role in popularizing skating in his country.

A very interesting feature of this essay is the first mention in literature of the outside forward loop three.

A few years later the same author published an essay on physical exercise, in which are mentioned the four edges, the change of edge, the Spread Eagle, a few numbers including the outside forward three, and detailed instructions for skating letters of the alphabet in large curves.

By this time, about 1795, the figure of a heart on one leg was universally known under its proper designation of 'three'. It is very probable too that the outside edge in the form of an eight was also then so called and these numerals, eight and three, no doubt suggested investigation into the completion of the other remaining basic numbers. This was carried still further in scratching names on the ice which seems to have become a real mania on the Continent in the early stages of figure-skating.

This seems to have been the main occupation of figure-skaters in Holland in the latter part of the eighteenth century. It was a great fascination and all sorts of intricate designs were made. It was a reaction to the monotonous Dutch roll, the long curves on the outside edge, that was really the entire repertoire of artistic skating in that country until then.

Skaters in Holland were divided into two factions: *Butenbeens-looper*, outside-edgers, and *Schuver*, shovers. The former aimed at elegance, the latter at pace. Artistic skating in Holland at the close of the eighteenth century did, however, make a step forward when complex figures exclusively performed on curves without turns were skated.

The eighteenth century marks the pioneer period when ice-skating as a real art was being born. Although a largish repertoire of graceful movements existed, especially as performed in England, they were not yet linked together, and so did not express any definite aim. With no real idea of interpretation, art in the sense of a final object of skill was non-existent. Skating first had to become a science before it could lay claims to being an interpretative art.

50

The Poets Sing its Praises

Sliding swiftly over a frozen surface gave excitement. Man, with the minimum of effort, could attain the speed of a galloping horse; this was both a thrill, and a feat that gripped the imagination in a period before speed became a common part of everyday life. Velocity in itself fascinated in particular the masses who limited their skating to careering over the ice in record time. But the charm of skating was in its poetic appeal, for it possessed something of the unreal in its motion. It opened up a field of delightful sensation, heretofore unobtainable. Skating gave a feeling of flying through space, like a bird resting on the wing before the wind. Gliding swiftly over the frozen surface and turning effortlessly here and there produced a sensuous feeling of abandon that seemed to have no object, no finality, yet was real and as such attracted the poets.

Addison and Thomson first sang its praises. Klopstock was one of the first who enjoyed it as a pastime. He became an expert skater and wrote an ode to skating. He encountered another poet on the ice, Johann Wolfgang von Goethe who also became proficient in the art. When they met, they did not discourse on verse but on skating—'the poetry of motion'. Klopstock found celerity of action its greatest charm. He discussed its fascination with Goethe and spoke of the merits of a long Friesland skate as being most suitable for speeding. Goethe on the other hand wore high grooved skates and enjoyed circling and turning. He was an artistic skater, a figure-skater of the eighteenth century. He grew passionately fond of skating, and found in this exercise such pleasure that he would forget his everyday worries. The hours he passed on the ice were never wasted, for he found in this exercise, this complete abandon, these 'aimless movements', as he put it, an awakening of noble thoughts. He owned that the hours passed in this way, seemingly lost and futile, aided the most rapid development of his poetical projects. This can be no exaggeration for his passion for skating was so great, that when dusk fell he could not always tear himself away from the ice, and under the moonlight he circled

51

on, deep in thought, and morning often broke with the poet still tracing the many figures of his imagination.

Goethe was also aware of the practical benefits that skating offered. In *Aus Meinem Leben* he refers to skating as 'an exercise which brings us into contact with the freshest childhood, summoning the youth to the full enjoyment of his suppleness, and is fitting to keep off a stagnant old age'. These three dimensions have never lost their attraction.

After Goethe came Lamartine who baptized skating as *l'exercise du nord*. He was no less fervent than his predecessor in his passion for skating. Even horses which he loved did not give the same satisfaction as the swift dream-like motion of travelling over a frozen lake. He even expressed a wish that winter with such pleasures would be eternal.

William Wordsworth loved skating too and practised it regularly in his native Lake District. It is claimed he was always the first out on the ice and could cut his name with skates.

Artistic skating had captured the imagination of hundreds during the eighteenth century. Its idyllic setting appealed in every walk of life and particularly to the poets—in this pioneer stage they contributed considerably to its development by singing its praises.

CHAPTER 6

Skating at the Beginning of the Nineteenth Century

A<small>T</small> the beginning of the nineteenth century ice-skating had become quite a general recreation in several countries in winter time.

About 1800 complex figures made entirely of curves were skated in the Netherlands and the fascination of scratching names and pleasing designs upon the ice with the point of the skate completes the picture of artistic skating in Holland. Figure-skating was to remain in this state in the Netherlands for more than a hundred years longer. The long flat blade of the Friesland running-skate was no doubt one reason why figure-skating remained undeveloped, for although it was possible to turn upon such a skate, it was not an instrument to inspire further exploration into the realm of threes and more complicated turns. But perhaps the main reason why artistic skating did not develop beyond a primitive stage in a country where opportunity was great as regards natural ice-rinks, was the invitation to speed which the frozen canals offered. These long stretches of ice tempted lengthy journeys in jovial company and the Dutch roll was all that was needed for such excursions. Furthermore skating here was a very useful means of locomotion. Skates replaced boats on the frozen canals.

In Germany, the Napoleonic wars were no doubt the main reason why artistic skating came to a standstill at the beginning of the nineteenth century. Skating was a recreation, an exhilarating exercise consisting of athletic movements that yielded pleasurable satisfaction, and even when practised vigorously it was limited to the basic elements of the art.

In England we have seen how artistic skating was greatly in advance of other countries in the middle of the eighteenth century. At that early period English skaters were concentrating their efforts on developing the crude outdoor exercise of sliding over the ice, Dutch rolling, into a real science. They concentrated upon the discovery of new curves and turns, on figure-skating as opposed to artistic skating. To the English, skating appealed more as an intriguing technique than as a graceful art. This scientific approach and emphasis on mathematical precision still remains the basic element of the English school today.

In the early part of the nineteenth century skating in England was practised by an increasing number of enthusiasts, which warranted a third reprint of Robert Jones's book in 1818. Yet while skating claimed more and more devotees, it does not appear to have made any further technical development since the first printing of his treatise nearly fifty years before. There is even some evidence that technically skating was degenerating, for about this time skaters were filling their pockets with a bag of lead-shot in order to learn the outside edge. The bag was placed in the pocket on the side to which they were to lean. Skating development in England at the beginning of the nineteenth century had come to a standstill.

In France, however, a significant evolution was taking place. The French temperament with its natural emphasis on the artistic was developing skating along similar lines. Further, its acceptance at the court of Louis XVI automatically made it a fashionable pastime almost exclusively in Paris and thereby assured its practice by all with pretence to elegance and manners. This meant that a special emphasis was placed on poise and grace, and these two fundamentals claimed for skating its place as an art in the true sense.

To the Parisian of taste, careering along the ice at speed bore a touch of vulgarity, and making long journeys over the frozen waterways did not demand any great skill for travelling in this fashion could be learnt very quickly. In Paris such a practice was not considered skating, 'sliding over the ice' was all they could call it, and they abandoned this to the less refined tastes of the Provinces.

The natural grace of the man of fashion, his poise and elegance, was transplanted to the ice. The result was a delightful lightness of the body when in movement over the ice. Gliding over such a smooth surface became almost poetic, swift turns and pirouettes were more graceful than spectacular, braking with elegance rather than abruptly. This stress upon the harmony of skating reiterates the preference of Stuart noblemen who performed the Dutch rolls with the elegance and taste of their standing as opposed to the rough and tumble of the people.

But since that time, nearly 150 years before, skating as a science had developed considerably and, at the beginning of the nineteenth century, possessed quite a varied repertoire of figures. Most of these figures and combinations as outlined in Robert Jones's book were first explored and put into practice by the English. During the greater part of the eighteenth century they were mainly concerned in creating a science out of a rough-and-tumble sliding on ice. Their natural temperament was more athletic than anything else and they developed skating on the lines of a sport, which had a hard 'forced' nature about it.

When transplanted to France, a radical change took place. It crossed the Channel with quite a small repertoire of curves and turns, and so was at a stage when a new creative impulse could give it further inspiration. The natural feline suppleness of the Latin, together with his artistic temperament, was just what was required at this stage of skating development. The English had created a science, the French were to develop it into an art.

The Gilets Rouges
Ice-skating had been imported into France in the reign of Louis XVI. When it was introduced it possessed all the curves and turns then known. By the beginning of the nineteenth century it had greatly changed—technically it possessed a much vaster repertoire of curves and turns and combinations. Artistically it had developed too, grace of movement had been added and was now an essential of skating.

At this juncture of ice-skating development it was the

55

aesthetic side that took on a very definite importance. Although the early pioneers of scientific skating in England had always stressed and attempted beautiful action in execution, grace where men were concerned was often interpreted as effeminate. As skating became more complicated, harmony of movement in difficult turns would be performed in the English manner, with style no doubt, but essentially athletically.

Skating in England in the days of its early formation as a science was a male occupation whereas it had been introduced into France as a pleasurable exercise in which both sexes could enjoy its delights, and although at this stage of skating development the male exponents dominated in number and in skill, the element of feminine charm was ever present on the ice. Grace, whether voluntary or involuntary was always there.

The striking characteristic of ice meetings in Parisian circles was their gaiety. The actual skating was often of a rough-and-tumble variety, and sometimes quite unorthodox in conception. Enthusiasm for this exhilarating exercise was becoming universal. Everyone who had seen skating wanted to try it—some were successful, some not.

There was the elegant count who in an unsuccessful turn fell and sprawled at the feet of his valet, a handsome colonel of the 'Grand Army' being lifted up by a simple soldier, the dandy, chilled somewhat by the cold, lorgnette to the eye, swerving here and there following the uncertain but charming gyrations of a beauty. There was the enthusiast who armed himself with a bamboo pole to help his balance and who, when losing control, would let fly his weapon which sometimes landed on the heads of nearby skaters or spectators. There was the grand and beautiful sleigh, its bow decorated by a magnificent silver swan, carrying a pair of distinction and pushed by two score lackeys, which careered across the ice taking all before it. There was also the wealthy skater who employed a dozen or more servants armed with sticks to descend upon the crowds and clear the way for an open run for their master.

Around the borders of the frozen surface this whirling scene was draped with tents and shelters in all colours, piles of snow decorated on the top formed the entrances to long alleys, single, double and sometimes triple for the purpose of speed-skaters. Travelling merchants with all kinds of wares wandered over the ice in search of business, around it all hundreds of spectators gathered, enchanted by this gay and colourful spectacle. An *élite* of skaters, known as *Gilets Rouges*, so named from their striking red waistcoats, would appear.

The *Gilets Rouges* were the first artists of skating. They stood out strikingly from the rest by their skill, their graceful execution of movements and their vivid appearance. They had at this early stage united all the essential elements in one. They were skaters in the true sense of the term.

Garcin's Notable Book

The appearance of the first book on ice-skating in the French language was a notable contribution to the art in many ways.

The author, J. Garcin, was very far in advance of his time and so his book remained for nearly forty years the supreme work upon the subject. It was a complete account of the most advanced stage of skating lore, and all the various figures and combinations were described in full.

Garcin was a fervent *Gilet Rouge*. He saw and found in skating a beautiful science. He studied it and helped to develop it technically, laying special emphasis upon the aesthetic side. He was in his heaven when executing graceful turns.

His choice of title for his book, *Le Vrai Patineur* ('The Real Skater') with the sub-title *How to Skate with Grace*, is significant.

Skating had now reached a point where it possessed a grammar and vocabulary that was used by a considerable percentage of enthusiasts on the ice, but a great majority of these were content with a careless execution of the movements.

So Garcin's book, besides its completeness about skating lore, aimed above all to impress upon the early enthusiast the aesthetic principles of the art. Throughout his book, when explaining the technical difficulties of a figure, he constantly

57

emphasizes the importance of executing it with grace and poise.

But the most striking fact of all about Garcin's work relates to the direct history of ice-skating in his having found it to be an art. Forty years previously Robert Jones had referred to it as such, but at that point in its story, the word 'art' was meant in a different sense. Skating in Jones's day was a noble exercise that had been reduced to an art, in other words, a method had been found to perform the various turns and curves with designed skill, and by following a regular system, it could be achieved with ease and safety. Art meant cleverness. Whereas Garcin and his fellow companions, the *Gilets Rouges*, elevated this 'technical' art to a 'tasteful' art.

The serious English skaters of Robert Jones's period did of course execute their turns with a harmonious movement of their arms and always attempted to perform all skating difficulties gracefully. They felt such action to be a vital part of the science.

But in Garcin's view skating was a complete art in itself, that possessed overwhelming qualities of skill and beauty that could be compared with the art of dancing, in fact he dedicated his book to no less a celebrity than Mlle Gosselen, *première danseuse* of the Imperial Academy of Music. It shows how much skating had progressed and how much Garcin believed in its future.

His book which is not only a reflexion of his own capacities and ideas as a skater but also a vivid portrait of the art in its most advanced stage till then, shows very definitely how skating was opening out into a wide field of development, which was much helped by technical progress, but also by the artistic outlook of the *Gilets Rouges*.

As in the time of the first real skaters in England of Robert Jones's day, Garcin and his companions felt space, and plenty of it, was needed for the interpretation of true skating. The discovery of new movements and turns required larger surfaces of ice.

Technically skating had made great advances in these forty years. The most significant of all, was that skating backwards was

no longer looked upon as something unnecessary and un-
pleasant, but was now considered a vital movement. Anyone
practising the art and unable to go backwards was only half a
skater. Garcin mentions that to make a fine reverse movement
drew greater admiration than when executing the same movement forwards.

This acceptance of propulsion backwards being a necessary
part of ice-skating is of primary importance after the Dutch
roll. It widened the field of action and with the Dutch roll was
one of the basic elements of ice-skating.

The backward outside and inside edges are fully described by
Garcin and together with the same edges forward form the pivot
of his book. Thirty-one figures follow, some combinations of the
above, others include pirouettes, jumps, steps and poses which
make up a considerable repertoire of ice-skating movements.
Many of these figures are described under highly fanciful
names. Reverence, Jump of Zephyr, Courtesan, Nymph, the
Adonis, Venus, the King of Rome, the Step of Apollo are a few
examples of an exaggerated artistic enthusiasm for normal
skating movements.

Garcin is mainly responsible for these names. He made the
first serious effort to give skating a language, which was not only
fitting from an artistic standpoint, but necessary technically.
With the invention of new steps, figures and combinations,
explanation of them became confused and difficult to memorize
when the few terms that existed then had continuously to be
repeated. In the names he chose, fine taste and elegance have
dominated, whereas more simple terms based on a technical
approach would appear to have been more natural and suitable.
But Garcin was first an artist in skating, and then a technician,
and every movement concerning its technique was visualized by
him as an artistic action. This was an exaggeration as the future
was to show, but Garcin was right in maintaining that skating
was an aesthetic science and therefore needed its own special
language to designate its subject-matter.

Explanations of the most important figures described in his

book will be found in the following chapter. It is sufficient to note here that the first chapters of his book deal very fully with the equipment of the skater, particularly the choice of skate and the method of fixing it to the boot. Before the first steps are made upon the ice he devotes several pages to the positions of the arms and a short note on the posing of the hands. Artistry is always dominant in Garcin's mind.

Then follows the description of the repertoire of figures with clear and useful suggestions of how to perform them correctly. He concludes his work with a chapter of interesting observations in relation to skating and skaters.

He hardly believes the stories that come from Holland and Germany of skaters writing their names upon the ice with their skates, but if allowing such things as being possible he certainly does not hold with such a practice, which is not in conformity with true skating aims. He touches upon correct behaviour and complete control when executing hazardous figures in a crowd. He also points out how skating can be learnt and enjoyed at all ages. A comprehensive glossary describing fully the technical terms of skating completes this outstanding book.

Skating in Garcin's Day
Of the thirty-odd skating figures described in Garcin's book, the *pas de huit*, the *Courtisane*, the *Nymphe* and the *Crochet* are the most outstanding new discoveries.

The *pas de huit* is the classic outside edge to a centre, and although known and practised in Robert Jones's day does not appear to have been regarded as an essential exercise.

Garcin found it to be the best drill for preparing a skater for the more ambitious combinations and the very fact that he gave it the simple name of 'eight' instead of a highly fanciful one, emphasizes the importance he attached to it as a basic exercise. Curiously enough it was considered a fairly advanced figure, and rarely attempted before long edges across the rink, pirouettes and turns had been mastered.

At the beginning of the nineteenth century the four classic

edges were practised in long flowing glides across the rink rather in the fashion of a free-skating movement. The inside edge forward was the first to be attempted. Because of this edge offering no difficulties in its execution, it was considered the most natural one and as taking precedence over the outside.

The manner of performing this figure was simple. A powerful run was made, and when sufficient speed was attained the skater glided quietly on to the inside edge taking up a relaxed position with arms outstretched but not stiff, one forward with the hand gracefully posed just above the head, the other falling gracefully behind, with the free leg and foot trailing elegantly.

The forward outside edge was performed in similar fashion and recognized as one of the most graceful skating movements. To master it was also considered a very big step towards the conquest of more difficult figures.

When skating in reverse the outside edge was the first to be attempted. Apart from the greater courage needed for its execution it was considered one of the best movements to show off the strength and handsome structure of the masculine body. Its execution was the same as for the forward edges and likewise for the inside back too, though this latter edge gave considerable difficulty in getting on to the inside and holding it.

A run was made backwards and when sufficient speed was attained, the skater rolled on to the inside edge lifting the other leg and trailing it behind. In order to make a long flowing edge to cover a large field of movement, a vigorous run backwards was necessary which handicapped somewhat the possibility of success in getting comfortably on to the back inside and holding it, so an alternative approach was made. The Spread Eagle, known as the *Révérence*, was used to enable the skater to get more easily on to the inside back and to control it. The skater glanced towards where he was going with his arms placed in the opposite direction, raised over his head with the palm of his hands facing outwards, and the fingers widely apart. In Garcin's poetic words, the effect produced was:

Like a Tragedian disturbed by terror,
Flees, in running back, an object full of horror.

There was also another variation in the interpretation of this edge, executed by merely changing the expression of the face. Therefore, instead of wearing a wild expression, the skater's face took on the aspect of one who was unable to hide the feeling in his heart with a gentle smile, and appeared to be rather reluctantly fleeing from an indiscretion. Garcin again sums up the effect as follows:

If by a haughty gesture I order you to flee,
The sweetness in my eyes forbids you to agree (obey).

From this rather amusing interpretation of the inside edge, a very striking point emerges. Using the expression of the face to aid interpretation of the figure was by no means superfluous, on the contrary it shows how the important artistic skaters in Garcin's day neglected nothing in order to produce a beautiful effect. They used every means towards creating a harmonious whole.

The four edges, practised then in long flowing glides, were recognized as the basis and pivot of skating. After the edges had been mastered and the skater was able to muster sufficient speed for executing long glides on all the edges, spins were the next figures to be learnt. They were generally used to terminate the outside edge. They were also employed to finish off aesthetically all the four edges.

It is very probable that the three turn known in Robert Jones's day was the forerunner of the pirouette very much in fashion in Garcin's time. Likewise the spin gave birth to the double and triple turns. Garcin called them hooks. It was the single hook or three turn that was employed to join up one skating movement with another. This simple turn was often called a half-spin and was considered a very graceful movement as well as an indispensable one. The spin, consisting of two or three revolutions, was used mainly to terminate a series of skating movements. It completed a small free-skating programme as it were, bringing the performance to an exciting finish. This pirouette was often placed between two distinct skating movements but it was never encouraged as it was considered ugly and out of place.

To the *Gilets Rouges* it broke the graceful flow. Its execution needed an abrupt stop, an interruption to gliding, and when completed, the next movement had to commence from standstill. It is more than probable that this dislike for placing a spin in the middle of a series of skating movements was because the pirouette in Garcin's day, very much in its infancy then, was not mastered and therefore uncontrollable, and in such circumstances would upset the elegance of the programme. The *Gilets Rouges* would never sacrifice grace.

Besides the outside forward eight already mentioned there were two other figures that were complete in themselves. The outside forward three known under the romantic name of *Courtisane*, and the back outside eight styled even more fancifully, the *Nymphe*. It is interesting to note that in the performance of these three circle figures, the skater repeated them several times keeping as far as possible to his original tracing. This was an unconscious step forward towards the basis of real figure-skating, for generally at that time when a skater had mastered a figure he performed it once and then went directly on to another. Repeating the same figure several times in the same place indicates that a new element, precision, was creeping into skating.

A further point of outstanding interest is revealed in the execution of the Jump of Zephyr, which is the simple three jump. It was considered perilous, but spectacular, and shows how skating had discovered an additional element in real 'athletics'.

Comedy too appears in the execution of 'the post boy stuck in the mud' which consisted of running backwards in a straight line and then making large steps as if to go forward but in reality standing still.

Two-footed movements included the beautiful Narcissus which was one foot placed in front of the other with the body leaning on the edge which the skater was travelling on, and the Crayfish was also popular, in which an eight was made to the centre on two feet by giving a strong twist with the hips. This latter movement passed as the most difficult performance in all skating. It was a forerunner of the Grape-vine, that popular two-footed combination of the beginning of this century.

There was also a combination called the Waltz that could be skated alone or with another skater, and consisted of a small forward outside edge with a spin of two revolutions on two feet, followed by a back outside edge. It was inspired from a folk-dance movement and is interesting because it suggests dancing on ice at this early stage. With a partner it was in the form of shadow-skating, both skaters executing identical movements side by side. However, it was found ungraceful when skated like this and it was no doubt because skaters then had not yet understood the possibilities of such an advanced theory, and therefore lacked sufficient skill in executing the figure in unison.

A primitive form of pair-skating also existed in which the Turtle-dove and the Garland were two popular movements. But the only real claim to pair-skating was in the touching of hands when the skaters came close, after executing an outside or inside edge forwards and backwards.

In Garcin's day skating was in full development. Many new figures had been acquired and athletic prowess had assumed a position of importance. Yet the most significant contribution bestowed upon skating then was the aesthetic deportment of the body.

CHAPTER 7

After Garcin

THE Garcin era with its considerable repertoire had brought skating to a point of advancement which under the circumstances of limited equipment can indeed be called 'notable'. Artistically it was more polished and technically more proficient.

Skating now seemed to have attained a point where further progress seemed impossible. It was a normal presumption, for the progress made during Garcin's era was considerable, and such an advance could not be expected to go on continuously. Skating at this point needed a breathing space to digest its accomplishments before developing further.

Its quite extraordinary evolution at the beginning of the nineteenth century in France was made possible by the driving spirit of one man, namely Garcin, whose enthusiasm and artistry made him a central figure around which the followers of skating, the *Gilets Rouges*, gathered to gain knowledge and inspiration.

We shall see during the course of this book how dominant personalities give a dynamic impulse which on each occasion has been little short of revolutionary. Garcin was the first of these.

Apart from his contribution to skating in the role of a performer and as a recorder of skating facts, his position as mentor to a skating *élite* at this early period was very important. Skating for the first time in its history possessed a nucleus, about which it could revolve, and from which constructive developments were possible.

It is worth while for the student of skating history to remember this point, for very shortly a new conflicting element was to be introduced.

C

During the next forty years the advancement of skating was due to a number of developments, a number of useful ideas which were to help skating considerably, but lack of method caused confusion, and no very constructive advances were made.

The position improved with the founding of the Skating Club in London.

The Skating Club

The Skating Club was founded in London in 1830. It is often erroneously referred to as the London Skating Club, but no such designation was ever given to it by its members who were proud to emphasize its title as being 'the' Skating Club.

The role it was to play from its foundation right through the nineteenth century was very great indeed. Paradoxically, it gave much and yet destroyed, or nearly succeeded in doing so by its attitude towards harmonious movement. This interesting point will be discussed fully in a later chapter, for although the subject belongs to the Skating Club's activities, it does not chronologically fit in here.

It was a select and rather exclusive club, with their Royal Highnesses the Prince and Princess of Wales and the Duke of Cambridge as its patrons. It was managed by a president, vice-president, committee and honorary secretary and governed by a code of rules. Permission was obtained from the Ranger of the Woods and Forests to erect the club marquee on the banks of that part of the Serpentine known as Long Water. On the stretch of ice that lay before this tent, members performed their repertoire of skating movements and figures. However during hard winters when all London thronged upon the ice, the reserved space before the tent was invaded by the enthusiasm of the general skating public who bumped and buffeted the distinguished members. Even the most stalwart could not resist this onslaught of rough, rowdy, and unskilled enthusiasts, and so they departed for other corners of the Serpentine. This flight has an important bearing upon the club's outlook on artistic skating. When its members were executing their graceful movements on their sacred stretch before their tent, it was the scene of an admiring crowd of spectators. They were fascinated by the skilled evolutions of these masters. When their reserve was invaded by other skaters the onlookers were under the impression they were watching the performance of the club members. Although there were among non-members, skaters who could perform a number of fine skating movements, these were rare exceptions, for the Skating Club boasted the most accomplished skaters in the country. The club regarded this misunderstanding as a slight on the skill of its members so it insisted they should always wear the badge of the club, a miniature silver skate hanging from a ribbon in their buttonhole. So no matter where they were upon ice, be it at Battersea Park, Wimbledon Park, Crystal Palace or Richmond Park, the distinctive sign dangling from the lapel of a member's coat would quickly confirm to the onlooker that he was watching the 'real thing'.

During the first years of the club's existence no examination was held for admission, although it was generally understood that no one would be admitted who did not possess a certain degree of proficiency. Admission was obtained by recommendation by members, and there was an honourable and gentlemanly agreement among these members not to propose a new member unless he was able to keep up the reputation for good skating, which the club had acquired.

The setting of a standard of high performance drew to its ranks a number of first-class skaters who were to play an important role during the middle of the nineteenth century in disseminating information on the art of skating to an ever-increasing public. Pooling their knowledge and sharing their inventions they were to carry skating development along at a great pace. The Skating Club then was functioning as it had been intended, it offered members a skating home, a citadel of skating thought. It guarded jealously its secrets and tabulated with pride the exploits of its most successful members, and so became an institution of authority in skating matters.

Its first contribution to skating progress was the popularizing

67

of 'combined-skating'. This was an intriguing aspect of skating in numbers, an English invention and remained a purely English manner of skating for nearly three-quarters of a century. It lingered on into the Edwardian era, but faded generally at the end of the century.

We shall see in a later chapter why English skating as it was termed was so important in the laying down of the basic principles of artistic skating. When a number of Englishmen gather together for the purpose of exercise, they instinctively think of a ball, either to kick, throw, hit or punch it, or run after it. In 1815 an Englishman put one on the ice for the purpose of making a stable centre, for the continuous execution of skating an outside edge and a three with a friend. This ball, later replaced by an orange, was to play a considerable role in the development of scientific skating. Previously, the performance of the then known basic figures was not practised over the same tracing. A skater was content to gracefully execute an outside edge here, and immediately go on to a three farther on, then a back edge and so on until he was tired or his repertoire became exhausted. Repetition of the same movement three or four times consecutively was not thought of, but was later practised in combined-skating.

The two skaters would start from the ball and describe a circle, say on the right outside edge. On completion of the circle they would arrive back at the ball, and then glide off on the other foot. This would be repeated two or three times and then a three would be performed and repeated. It can at once be seen that it had not the primitive ingredients of pair-skating as practised by the Dutch two centuries before, it had more the aspect of a game. Much skill was needed for control and the whole idea was conceived as a combination of technique and sport. This was more in keeping with the more practical demands of the English skater than the artistic approach of the French.

The Skating Club was founded by those whose interest in combined-skating was foremost in the club's early years.

The Skating Club was the first permanent centre of skating thought—the first unofficial institution of skating, apart from the earlier but dissimilar Edinburgh Club.

Mr Boswell's Skate

Real progress in the development of skating had come to a standstill after Garcin's era. With all the ideas that were conceived by members of the Skating Club in the 1830s it was not possible to put them into practice without changing the primitive skating equipment at their disposal. A better skate was needed. Improvements had been made to the skate in general, but they were unimportant alterations, the blade remained unchanged.

It was a Mr Henry Boswell, a resident of Oxford, an enthusiastic and brilliant skater for the period, who skated outside edges forwards and backwards, single and double threes and primitive forms of loops with skill and courage, who found it absolutely necessary to improve upon the skate-iron if such figures were to be executed with ease and safety.

In those days the art of sliding over the ice was referred to as 'forward and back skating'. It was a distinction of importance, for it was not only considered to require more skill when skating backwards, but it needed much courage to perform such a feat on the skates then in use.

The iron blade of the skate that projected beyond the toe to finish in a flourishing curve before the front of the boot, only reached the beginning of the heel, where it stopped abruptly, squared at a sharp angle.

Such a blade, fixed as it was in an exaggerated forward position in its wooden frame, demanded of the skater a forward lean. It was little removed from the speed-skate, which, even if far from the ideal, was at least more suited to their sport than the other was to artistic skating.

Forward skating was comparatively easy and circles and three turns were possible to a skater that possessed the necessary skill, but when it came to skating backwards it was another story. It could be done and was done quite artistically in Garcin's day, but it was difficult and uncomfortable to perform, and dangerous.

Such a skate with the heel of the foot only partially supported, and the blade cut short at the back could not always glide over even slight impediments that might be on the ice surface, such as small stones, grit and leaves. The skate would stop dead and a fall inevitably follow. Although it was the period of spills and rough-and-tumble experiment, dangerous falls could only be avoided if the skater leant very much forward. Attempts to skate backward edges, double threes and loops in such exaggerated and uncomfortable positions could only be made under great difficulty. Real progress was therefore checked.

This was the reason Mr Boswell turned his attention in 1836 to a new form of skate-iron. After experimenting with other enthusiasts at Oxford with irons of different lengths and different curves, he finally achieved the following result. He cut off the projecting toe-piece and extended the blade the whole length of the boot, thus giving the heel full support. Toe- and heel-ends of the iron were rounded off. This model of skate would enable skaters to carry out all possible turns and twists, and blades of this shape were in use in England for more than sixty years.

Mr Boswell took this revolutionary pattern to a Birmingham maker and had some four dozen pairs of irons made. These were acquired by enthusiasts in Oxford and as a result of the improved skate the sport became increasingly popular. Rapid progress was made in skating, and a club was formed in 1838, the members being principally mechanics, tradesmen and College servants, and combined-skating was introduced.

The figures consisted of circles and parts of circles, of outside and inside edges, worked round a common centre varied by the cross-roll and threes.

The club was known as the Oxford Society and its great aim was to perform combined-skating with clockwork precision. This emphasis on accuracy was another step forward and was made possible by the improved skate-iron, which was in such demand that a Sheffield firm took up its manufacture, and they came into general use. These skates with their long blades and rounded ends became known as club skates, presumably taking this name from the Oxford Club.

Mr Boswell played a dominant role in this skating society where his technical experiments were not limited to the improvement of the iron, for he designed many combination-figures of great simplicity and effectiveness that long held their own. He finally became a professional and came to London performing at the Coliseum on artificial ice.

During a lifetime devoted to skating he had contributed much towards its popularization as a sport by his performances on ice, but it was the skate he invented that gives him a place of honour in the annals of skating. Skating now had a fitting tool to work with.

The Work of Cyclos

During this period of development all the achievements made by the experimenters upon the ice, wherever skating was practised, were to be recorded for the first time in a book called *The Art of Skating* by 'Cyclos', the pseudonym of George Anderson, for many years President of the Glasgow Skating Club. The first printing was published in 1852 and marks the next chapter forward in skating literature after Garcin's work nearly forty years before. Other books in French and English had been published in the meantime, and one particularly, *The Skater's Manual*, 1831, was an excellent little work for its date, adding a number of new figures, double threes forward and backward, and listed thirteen combined-figures.

In France the published works and pamphlets at this time were mostly dilutions of Garcin's book, adding nothing of importance to what he had written. In Germany, C. S. Zindel issued a book called 'Skating' (*Der Eislauf*, 1825) but again practically nothing new was added to what was already known in that country at the turn of the century.

Cyclos's work, including his second edition, published under his own name in 1868, set down a few additional figures that even if they had been skated sometime before, had never been recorded.

This was the period when changes of edge were being exploited to the full. The continuous Serpentine Line, now known as the Sea Serpent, changing the edge from out to inside repeatedly on the same foot, was practised in Robert Jones's day, and was a favourite then. In the 1850s it was not indulged in so much, being considered rather a freak movement, but it was the foundation of a more advanced branch of skating. It made possible the execution of the 'Q' figures, which are today no longer fashionable, but they were stepping-stones to all the modern three-circle figures and paragraphs.

The simple 'Q' figure consisted of a right outside forward, a change to right inside, followed by a three on the outside edge back; after this circle had been completed, the figure was finished and showed the tracing of the letter 'Q' on the ice. The Shamrock was the outside forward reverse 'Q'. Its tracing displayed three circles upon the ice in the shape of a shamrock about two-thirds completed. A deep full three was made and after completing the inside back circle, the edge was changed to the outside and the figure terminated by a complete outside back circle. It was looked upon as a difficult and beautiful figure. When this backward edge of the Shamrock had been mastered it was possible for the skater to execute the United three, in reality the forward and backward three. Then followed the Canadian eight which needed the same change of edge and was the back eight on one foot.

These figures were all adapted to combined-skating and it can be seen at once how the change of edge was the essential movement for its progress. Without it, there could have been no development.

Forward loops in a primitive form and mentioned as of Canadian origin were also new figures described in Cyclos's book. As performed then they represented a broken spin rather

72

more than a modern loop. The procedure was to take an outside forward edge, turn a loop, come out of it, go into another and then finish with a half-circle before going off on to the other foot.

The contribution to skating development of real importance in Cyclos's work was his approach to the subject. He did not just collect all the known figures and movements and set them down in encyclopaedic fashion. This would have been a considerable contribution in itself, but he began to put order in the quickly growing repertoire of skating science—he started to reduce the figures to a system.

He began with two-footed movements, finding them the simplest and believing them to be the first steps for a solid basis. Then came the single foot forward movements, followed by single foot backwards and finally figures which were combinations of threes and changes of edge. Combined-figure movements completed the order.

His book was translated into German where it appears to have been instrumental in reviving skating interest in that country which had been dulled since the outbreak of the Napoleonic wars. It was published there two years after the first English edition.

In Sweden it became the first skating textbook in its Swedish translation.

Pleasures and Dangers of Skating

In the middle of the nineteenth century skating was indulged in wherever a sheet of ice could be found. It was not, however, practised always as seriously as we have seen was the case in Oxford and at the Skating Club in London. In comparison to the enormous number of skaters everywhere, the numbers in these select societies were very small indeed, and apart from them and the descendants of the *Gilets Rouges*, skating was still very much the thrill of sliding over slippery surfaces.

France where the creation of novelties has always been strong, was very much to the fore in inventing apparatus and ideas for getting the most out of fun on the ice. Some of these had no impact upon real skating, and are only mentioned here because they helped widely to popularize sliding over ice, and so indirectly spread the growth of skating.

One of these was particularly quaint. It consisted of a chair set high above the ice upon a wooden board, from which projected an iron bar on each side to taper downwards and form a runner upon which the whole contraption rested. Seated in the chair the occupant was able to propel himself over the ice by means of a short pole which he plunged through a hole in the board. This vehicle was extremely popular.

Sleighs filled with numerous people and pulled and pushed by skaters had been seen on the ice in the early Dutch days and on the Thames more than a century before, but what was new and striking was the presence of a speaker who rode standing in the sleigh and recited verses of poetry to charm its occupants and add to the spell of the glide.

The use of sleighs with sails whose locomotion was aided by a crew wielding long poles and prodding the ice was mainly a masculine occupation. It was an ice-sport.

But the biggest thrill on ice at this time was undoubtedly the 'slippery dip'. A tall tower was constructed at the edge of the ice border, and from its high platform a steep wooden slope, sprinkled with water and frozen hard, descended to the natural ice-field below. The most courageous of skaters mounted to the top of the tower by a ladder, put their skates on, then descended the precipitous slope at speed, some on two feet, some on one, to continue their run along the ice-field as long as the momentum lasted. This definitely was the means of getting the utmost out of the primitive idea of sliding effortlessly over the ice. The steep descent gave a sensation of flying like a bird through space, something which man had long envied but never could do. The swift glide over the ice at the end was an exhilarating thrill.

In England ice-contraptions were not only for the enjoyment of ice-sports but some were 'self-helps' for learning to skate.

The most notable of these useful instruments, designed exclusively for forward skating, was invented by Cyclos. It was especially recommended to ladies who were timid of the ice, to give them confidence, correct attitude and regularity in striking. It consisted of a wooden frame, in the form of two triangles with a bar joining them breast-high for the hands to grasp, and another bar close to the ice to prevent the learner's skates from going too far forward and causing a fall. The frame did not rest upon iron runners but upon simple planks of wood. This was to avoid moving the frame too easily, which would fail to teach the necessity of keeping the feet at right angles, the only position to gain pushing power. It was the same principle as the pushing of a chair across the ice, a common scene in those days. But a chair was ill-balanced and falls were frequent with it. Cyclos's simple frame was a studied instrument that took into consideration all the pitfalls a beginner was likely to encounter.

There was other equipment a skater might find necessary as a precautionary measure. A ladder and a rope were generally taken by a prudent party of skaters, and a lone skater often carried a longish stout pole with him, so in the event of ice giving way beneath him, he had the means of extricating himself.

In those days when a frost came the first question was 'Will the ice bear today?' It was advisable to have a certain knowledge of ice conditions.

Death by drowning when skating was by no means unheard of, and generally occurred on thin ice over a fast-running stream—when the ice broke over a deep brook and the skater fell in, and unable to get a grip upon the breaking ice, was carried beneath the surface and imprisoned. Not even a party of friends was guaranteed to be able to get hold of and extricate the skater from such a position.

When a skater felt the ice was breaking under him one method adopted to avoid going under was to fling himself forward on his face and try to creep on to sounder ice. During this process he was recommended not to cry out for aid, for the sound of his voice was thought likely to rupture the ice further!

To know how to get out of a hole in the ice was equally important to a skater as being able to perform the outside edge.

Dangers were certainly many, but the pleasures were greater and at this point it seemed nothing could hinder progress in the pleasures of ice-sports.

CHAPTER 8

Skating on the American Continent

ICE-SKATING had been practised in North America during the eighteenth century and although it is very difficult to decide who introduced it there, it is more than probable it was through the medium of British army officers, who early indulged in skating as an exercise. Philadelphia was one place where ice-skating was enjoyed by the British officers stationed there during the middle of the eighteenth century. Colonel Howe, brother of General Howe of Revolutionary fame, was a leading exponent. These men inspired the youth of the city to take to sliding over the ice—one of the first American skaters of note as early as 1760 was Benjamin West, an artist who became President of the Royal Academy.

He came to Europe, first to Rome when he was twenty-three and was the subject of much interest, being the first American painter to visit that city. When he was twenty-five he visited London. One day when strolling through St James's Park he watched the skaters on the canal, hired a pair of skates, and joined them on the ice. Bustled here and there by the crowd he was noticed by a gentleman skater who was impressed by West's style, and was informed that there was better skating over in Kensington Gardens. So later, while skating there he bumped into his old acquaintance Colonel Howe, who asked him to give a demonstration of the Philadelphia style of skating. In company with Howe were some noblemen who were in turn impressed by West's skill and sense of style. The news spread and within a few days many men about town came with the crowds to see the novelty of an American skater.

West is cited as having performed the Salutation with skill and fine grace. It was considered an advanced figure, and indicates that skating on the American continent in the middle of the eighteenth century was in full development. West's own proficiency confirms this.

At about the same time ice-skating was very probably introduced into Canada through the medium of British army officers as in the USA. This was before the introduction of fashionable skating in France, and there is no evidence that the French ever practised it in Canada except in a most primitive way. The frozen rivers and lakes offered enormous opportunities for the simple practice of sliding as a means of 'getting somewhere' and the French army had knowledge of its usefulness since in Europe a century before the famous French Marshal Catinat harassed by the Dutch, who used skates to effect lightning raids upon his troops across the Scheldt, ordered iron blades for his soldiers, so they could pursue and annihilate the enemy bands.

Skating therefore as in the USA was introduced as a pleasing and fashionable exercise. It very probably was practised first in Canada in the region of Nova Scotia when the British took over this part of Arcadia from the French in 1713.

Later explorers, hunters, fur-traders and settlers appear to have kept a pair of skates in their equipment apart from snow-shoes as a means of locomotion over the frozen rivers and lakes, and stories are told how some of them owe their lives to their skill and speed on the irons in fleeing from Red Indians.

Skating was well established on the North American continent by the beginning of the nineteenth century, and we shall see in the next episodes of this chapter, how quickly it developed and how useful were its contributions.

The First All-metal Skate
By the middle of the nineteenth century Philadelphia had become an important skating centre and it was in that city around 1848 that the first all-metal skate was made.

It was the invention of E. V. Bushnell. Both blade and footplate were made of iron. It was the commencement of a general improvement in the skate, and particularly the skate fixture.

When Boswell lengthened the blade to run the whole length of the boot he formed the basis of the modern skate. But the improvement concerned the blade only, the manner of fixing the skate to the boot had not yet been solved. Cumbersome and untidy straps were still the principal means of holding the skate to the boot. It was never very satisfactory, especially with the diverse uses to which skates were being put.

Even Bushnell's skate used straps to begin with—as many as four of them, the first two near the toe, the third to support the instep, and the fourth at the front of the heel. Very soon after the invention the straps were dispensed with, and a better idea evolved. The skate was to be fastened tight to the boot by means of clamps.

The skater now had a much more efficient fastening that allowed him to perform twists and turns with less danger of the skate coming loose from the boot. He also could now attempt more extravagant movements, abrupt stops and such twists as put strain on the skate without the risk of straining the ankle or of having a bad fall caused by the foot slipping away from the skate. The whole instrument was much stronger, and the skate remained attached to the boot, both now forming a whole.

This permanent fastening of skate to boot was very important—by its rigidity it gave real security and, combined with Boswell's extension of the blade, was to produce the first real skate capable of executing the most difficult figures with an ease and precision, although skate design was to develop very much further before the modern skate was evolved.

Curiously enough this idea of permanent fastening of the skate to the boot was not new. As far back as 1697 the Czar of Russia, Peter the Great had a pair of Dutch skates made for him and permanently fastened to the boot which he used at Zaandam in Holland.

That this idea was not adopted, and not even attempted by skaters at that period seems somewhat odd, but it might be explained as being considered just another extravagance of the great monarch. As there is no record of his prowess on the ice,

79

it is very probable he was not very skilled, and a bad performance might very well be put down to the inefficiency of his skates.

The all-metal skate from Philadelphia started off a new wave of enthusiasm for skating, and the skate itself became for the first time a speculation among manufacturers for quick profits. A few years later Germany was rivalling the Americans in skate production and selling them all over the world where skating was practised. Models, good and bad, to suit all tastes, were to be had. As many as 200 patterns of skate were on the market in America and Europe around 1865. Their variations were mainly in the manner of fastening. Clamping permanently the skate to the boot was not yet accepted universally, nor was it considered by all skaters then to be the perfect solution.

The Philadelphia Skating Club
Deep winter was often interrupted by short spells of thaw followed by rain, which covered with water the various ponds and small lakes which surround Philadelphia. One night was often sufficient to freeze the last layer of rain and afford next morning some splendid stretches of new ice. When a frost was long and severe the Schuylkill River froze and skating could be enjoyed by hundreds from Fairmont Dam to the Falls.

There were many favourable opportunities for sliding on ice for everybody living in the city, but the tradition of fine skating laid down by the British army officers a century before at the time of Benjamin West continued. The frozen sheets of water in and around Philadelphia always had real skaters upon them. So a club was formed in 1849, the first in the United States.

It was styled the 'Skating Club of the City and County of Philadelphia' and in 1861 it joined forces with the Humane Society and became the 'Philadelphia and Humane Society'. The collaboration appears necessary and suggests how dangerous and difficult it was for ice-enthusiasts of the last century to pursue their favourite pastime. This was done on the Schuylkill River, and falling through the ice and being drowned was by

16. A CLUB FIGURE. Skating in the English style at the turn of the century

17. DUTCHMEN SKATING WITH POLE. A novel method used by the Dutch for skating against the wind. The second skater, who was sheltered, helped the leader along on the tandem principle. When sliding with the wind, the skaters ran side by side holding the pole over their shoulders

a. Four-point star.
THEODOR LANGER 1882

b. ALEX. LEBEDEFF 1883

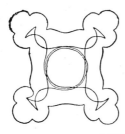

c. IVAR HULT 1888

d. G. SANDERS 1892

e. GUSTAV HÜGEL 1894

f. N. PANIN 1897

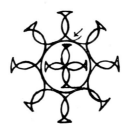

g. A. CUMMING 1908

18. SPECIAL FIGURES. Figures made by champions of the period 1880–1910

19. (left) ULRICH SALCHOW, 1901. The great Swedish skater dominated competitions at the beginning of the century, and still holds the unbeaten record of nine European and ten World Championship wins

20. (right) MRS EDGAR SYERS, 1906. First Ladies' Champion of the World and runner-up to Salchow when she competed in the men's event of 1902

21. (left) LILY KRONBERGER OF HUNGARY. First skater to attempt an entire free-skating programme to music

22. (right) CHARLOTTE. Shown performing the celebrated 'fade-out' that concluded her exhibition programmes

23. HAND-IN-HAND SKATING. This followed on from roller-skating and came into vogue at the beginning of the century. It is a forerunner of modern ice-dancing

24. MR AND MRS T. D. RICHARDSON OF ENGLAND. They pioneered shadow-skating in the Olympic skating events in 1924, thereby enriching pair-skating

no means uncommon. In those days members were obliged to carry little wooden reels attached to the left wrist and containing a length of strong thin rope. Some skaters placed this in their skating-bag and carried it in their hands as they skated, dropping it at a convenient spot where they wanted to indulge in figure-skating. It was sometimes used as a centre and so always near at hand and ready to be thrown to an unfortunate comrade who had broken through the ice. It was the means of saving many a life. The annals of the club not only record the skating triumphs of their members, but many heroic rescues.

Dress was also an important factor, and like the *Gilets Rouges* uniformity was essential, and up till 1865, the top hat, swallow-tailed coat, pantaloons, and white tie were the official costume for figure-skating in the club. One of the most skilful members who believed dress was very important to the elegant art of skating, appeared in evening dress with the coat tightly fitting and buttoned.

The club repertoire of figures consisted of forward rolls, forward and backward threes, the Grape-vine, the cross-foot spin, variations of 'Q' figures and the Philadelphia twist, which was a complicated Grape-vine. Members who performed these figures skilfully and gracefully would generally have a retinue of boys and girls following in their wake admiring their dexterity. Sometimes a crowd of several hundred people would form a circle round these good skaters watching their gyrations. The thick crowd concentrated in one spot was often the cause of the ice cracking, when there would be a hurried scramble to firm land.

The Philadelphia Skating Society was at this time the source of stimulation in the United States. Skating was practised as an art there and so obtained a high degree of skill and execution that inspired. Many of its members emigrated to Washington and particularly New York, which was growing fast. They soon sought out ponds or any stretch of water that froze and could be skated on, and they spread the art of skating up and down the East Coast.

81

North American Contributions to the Art

Skating was very quickly taken up by other cities. New York in particular, which formed its club in 1863, soon became an important skating centre. Among the initial 150 members were some of the best American skaters of the day, skate designers, skate manufacturers, inventors and dealers. Such wealth in skating interests amassed in a whole, was bound to produce useful contributions to its progress.

It was in America at this time, and especially in the New York club, that the design and fastening of the skate was experimented on to the full and improvements made, which were in advance of Europe. This allowed the American skaters to indulge in a quantity of intricate figures and completely new movements which for some time were to be regarded in other countries as the American school of skating. Very shortly after their invention they were to become international and copied in particular by the Viennese and other Continental countries.

They were one- and two-footed movements including acrobatic feats not belonging to real skating art, and their attraction lay in the design they cut upon the ice, and we know the fascination the writing of names on ice held for the skaters in the eighteenth century. It would be natural for a skater, seeing the lines he made upon fresh ice, to try tracing his name or that of a girl friend, and it has been said that even a declaration of love was once thus engraved upon the ice.

It must be understood that to be able to perform such a feat, a rigidly held skate was absolutely necessary to be able to withstand the violent twists and jerks entailed. The American idea of clamping the skate to the boot opened up new fields in this domain and so skaters in New York, Philadelphia and Boston indulged in gymnastic movements on one foot and created intricate designs of stars, half-moons and flowers upon the ice. When resketched upon paper they were extremely beautiful to look at, but the actual execution of them upon the ice often looked very ugly, with sometimes brutally abrupt movements. They really held no place in the art of pure skating and must be classified in the category of stunts. Yet these feats of gymnastic skill held sway amongst skaters for more than half a century and in the late 1890s formed an important part of the major international competitions.

Superior skate fittings were also valuable aids to Canadian enthusiasts in working out new movements in advance of Europeans. The Grape-vine, from which many variations were later evolved, was executed with two feet upon the ice, and is of Canadian origin. The feet remain in line toe to heel, and by swaying the body, the feet interlace as they move along; a half-spin was sometimes added and then the original movement continued. Grape-vines were to capture the imagination of skaters and the better skaters included variations of them in their free programmes until the 1930s. After the turn of the century they were not only a fashionable feat, but considered the hall-mark of a skilful skater. Performed in their entirety they do not really belong to classic skating, but they have their place. The modern skater has adapted part movements of two-foot Grape-vines in placing them as links in a chain of steps.

It was in Canada that the first covered rinks appeared. They came into existence around 1860 when the skating vogue was at its height. The idea evolved because the long continued frosts which allowed skating for considerable periods at a time were often spoiled by the heavy downfalls of snow. So large sheds, called 'ice-rinks', were constructed over sheets of natural ice, and gave the skater for the first time the possibility of exercising in comfort under conditions that remained the same from day to day, free from wind and snow, in all weathers except thaw.

They were gas-lit, so skating, which was often practised by moonlight under dangerous conditions in the unsheltered ponds, could be indulged in on the ice-rink whether there was a moon or not with complete safety, as there was always someone in attendance in case of an accident.

These sheds guaranteed the Canadian skater a three-months season, and they were the scenes of elaborate fancy-dress balls, the forerunners of the great Canadian ice-carnivals of today.

83

CHAPTER 9

Jackson Haines

THE memory of the outstanding American skater, Jackson Haines, is kept alive in modern skating by the classic sitting spin which he invented and which is included in every ambitious skater's repertoire. But that was not his only contribution to the art of skating. In the late 1860s he crossed Europe leaving a trail of enthusiasm for the excellence of his exhibition-skating in many countries. Mere demonstrations of technical skill would of course not have been sufficient to warrant the triumphs he achieved nor the popularity he enjoyed amongst the highest society; he was also an outstanding artist, and it is by his being so rather than his inventive spirit, that his claim to fame is to be estimated.

There are still doubts about the real birthplace of Jackson Haines. Chicago claims him and so does Troy, NY. There are reasons to believe he was born in Canada, but whatever may be correct, one thing is sure, he was a North American skater. He was born around 1840, the son of a cabinet-maker, and in his tenth year went to Europe with a relative in order to become a dancer. On the wish of his father, who it is believed wanted his help to carry on the family business, the young Jackson returned to the United States. But the call of the stage was too strong for Haines, and at the age of seventeen he left home to study for a theatrical career. It was during this period of apprenticeship that he acquired a real appreciation of dramatic values that were to serve him in good stead in his skating successes.

But it was particularly in dancing that he worked so hard. He skipped meals in order to pay for a large mirror which he placed against the wall in his room to observe himself in it and study the movements of the body and the positions of the limbs. He

84

thus developed fine bodily grace and it would be about this period that he found in skating, as Garcin had before him, an affinity with ballet dancing—he appreciated and understood the vast possibilities of skating.

He worked on the ice with the same enthusiasm he put into ballet, and placed more value upon the pose of the body and the positioning of arms and legs than upon the figures he skated. He gave exhibitions up and down the East Coast and Canada and although the general public received him with great enthusiasm, certain skating circles criticized his exaggeration in pose and lack of figure-skating technique.

He never abandoned this emphasis on pose, but after severe criticism of his skating technique he set to work to improve this deficiency. So seriously did he take this, that he is said to have practised his sitting spin for nine years before he was satisfied with it.

But first he was to invent a new skate particularly suited to his purpose. The blade was forged on to the toe- and heel-plates, which could be directly screwed on to the sole and heel of the skating boot. This was a skate that was solid and reliable, that would allow a free-skating performance by Haines to be carried out without any danger of technical breakdown on the part of the instrument used. This skate with its turned-up toe was elegant to look at and typified all Haines's work on the ice by blending both beauty and technical skill. The skate served as a model for nearly seventy years.

During the Civil War he appears to have varied his accomplishments as opportune. Sometimes he was on the stage in a juggling act, swinging Indian clubs, sometimes an exhibition-skater, a teacher of physical culture and finally a ballet master. But as the Civil War lingered on, such occupations were destined to suffer, and with business as a ballet master practically at a standstill, Jackson Haines left the United States in 1864 for Europe.

He first visited England and gave a number of skating exhibitions, but did not impress the Victorian skating circles. His posing and theatricalism shocked when compared with the rigid manner of skating the English indulged in at that period. It was considered 'fancy skating' and this was meant disparagingly.

He then went to Stockholm and there began his triumphal skating tour of the capitals of North and Central Europe. Wherever he skated he aroused frenzied enthusiasm. But it was only in one city, Vienna, that he found understanding as well as admiration. This musical city first took him to its heart, then followed him on to the ice with its dances, and waltzed with him to the fascinating rhythm of Strauss. He left an indelible impression upon the Viennese ice-skating society, inspiring them and instructing them. This undoubtedly began the 'Vienna school of skating' that was in turn to evolve into the system known as the 'international style', which is the early expression of free skating proper.

For several years he toured the Continent giving skating exhibitions on single rollers, and on ice. He always skated alone and appeared in the greatest variety of costumes, sometimes as a Russian, then a fairy prince, or disguised as a lady, and even a polar bear. These theatrical costumes, his skating skill, bodily grace and fine musical interpretation made him one of the great showmen of the day. He also stunted with stilts on the ice. As such he became an international celebrity and was a guest at several courts in Europe and it is said became a fast friend of the Czar Alexander II.

While he was alive his fame was such that rinks were not only named after him but built for him, and children were christened after him. He was the first international figure in ice-skating and because of that alone, skating as an art was to become better known and appreciated.

His dazzling career appears to have come to an abrupt stop about 1875, very probably through failing health, for it seems he passed the last years of his life peacefully in Scandinavia where he contented himself with instructing. He died in 1879 when he was probably thirty-nine years of age in the small Finnish town

of Gamla-Karleby. Upon his tomb is the simple inscription:
'*Jackson Haines—The American Skating King.*'

The Work of Jackson Haines

The triumph that Jackson Haines enjoyed as an exhibition-
skater in Europe was due to a number of factors. He arrived on
the Continent at a time when ice-skating was quite unimpressive
and little developed as a spectacular art, and so he electrified the
skating world by his revolutionary interpretation of sliding
over ice and he conquered the general public by his theatricalism and showmanship. The serious skater had not visualized
such a stagy approach to skating, and the ordinary spectator
witnessed a new type of entertainment which pleased and thrilled.
Adding to this a magnetic personality, it can be understood how
he went from success to success as he travelled from one capital
to another. His career was meteoric.

As time wore on the name of Jackson Haines became known
as that of the founder of the international style of skating, which
is the type of skating art practised throughout the world today.
Although it must not be exaggerated, the part played by him in
the story of skating was of great importance, and he was undoubtedly the forerunner of a great development.

Jackson Haines brought into skating more art than science.
It was exactly what was needed, for when he arrived in Europe
it was developing upon the lines of elegant mathematical outdoor exercises. It was of course a necessary part of its growth,
the actual scientific basis upon which the art could be built.
English skaters, and particularly translations of Cyclos's book
or parts of it, no doubt played a large part in influencing skating
on the Continent.

Jackson Haines is supposed to have scoffed at the small figures
skated by members of the New York Skating Club. He certainly
did not believe that the practice of figures to centres represented
either the peak or ideal of skating. He certainly did not neglect
the opportunity when in England of learning the latest turns and
twists they were busy inventing for their combination-skating

87

to a centre. He understood the importance of skating the edges, changing them, and turning the threes to a centre, but he believed them to be only a necessary step towards skating proper.

His long graceful spirals were often interrupted by lightning twists of the body that at once surprised and captivated the onlooker. He gyrated at high speeds and leapt from the ice to appear almost flying. He performed all his movements with a wonderful sureness and executed his most difficult figures with equal ease, and removed any impression of danger in skating.

He realized that space was also required. Speed, poise, athletic skill and beauty of movement, which he believed to be the basis of skating could only be shown to advantage over a large surface of ice. He wore colourful theatrical costumes to emphasize the individuality of his numerous turns and enriched them with musical accompaniment.

With these means he revolutionized the then accepted outlook on skating, by creating an art and yet popularizing it.

The Echo of Jackson Haines

It was quite natural that such an outstanding personality in skating as Jackson Haines would leave behind him a trail of admirers and pupils to carry on and consolidate his ideas, and it was in the creation of the 'Viennese school', of which he was unquestionably the inspiration and indirectly the founder, that this took greatest effect. It was in this gay city of dancing and music where he enjoyed his greatest triumphs, but where—more important than personal glory—his ideals in skating were understood.

When he arrived in Vienna in 1865, the town was 'dancing crazy'. After seeing Jackson Haines gracefully swinging over the ice, interpreting a waltz, a march, a mazurka and a quadrille in rhythmic movement, they followed him and took their own dances and their music on to the ice. The former ballet dancer had awakened these musically gifted Viennese to the possibilities offered by this new outdoor winter pastime.

During the time he spent in Vienna he had many pupils, some

of them not only learning his skating figures and movements, but also copying his mannerisms and even his costumes. One of them was Leopold Frey, who resembled Haines, and set himself the task of imitating his master in detail! He was a very gifted skater and in 1882 won the 'Great International Skating Tournament' in Vienna, receiving as first prize a statuette of Jackson Haines, which was the work of one of the city's leading sculptors.

Another brilliant pupil of Haines was Franz Belazzi, a born show-skater. It was perhaps this particular aptitude that made him Haines's favourite. When he was seventeen he partnered his master in exhibitions in Vienna and Prague, and on these occasions Haines skated at the same time as Belazzi.[1] After an introduction together each one performed his own programme and on its conclusion both skaters joined in the centre and executed a jump or two, terminating with a Viennese waltz of Haines's invention. The second half of the programme was exclusively theatrical. Haines appeared as a bear and Belazzi as his trainer. The scene was a village square. Thunderous applause greeted the skaters when the exhibition ended with the bear waltzing with the young trainer. Belazzi continued to play an important role in skating in Vienna even when at nearly eighty years old he was on the board of the Engelmann Ice-rink.

Among Jackson Haines's most ardent disciples was Diamantidi who was a great believer in theory. It was Haines's mastery of skating that impressed him. His lightning turns performed with ease and beauty of movement could only be performed in Diamantidi's estimation by adhering to the basic scientific figures. Mastering these, the skater was ready to interpret in his own personal manner, like Haines did, the higher expression of the art which included spirals, spins and jumps. So after Haines had left the skating scene he worked on this principle and in collaboration with others of Haines's students, Von Korper and Max Wirth, elaborated a system of figures, simple and complicated, and in 1881 presented it to the skating world in a club

[1] One of the rare occasions on which Haines gave an exhibition with another skater.

production called *Spuren auf dem Eise*. It was a great contribution to the science of skating, for in it was drafted the international style, evolved by the Vienna school, and it set the skating world a standard. At that stage it was not technically perfect, but the model was set and it was the right one. Its continued inspiring influence and notable contributions made between 1881 and the outbreak of the Second World War represents a very large part in the evolution of the modern skating story. It was Vienna that inspired, and in a way this Vienna school is the most enduring monument of Jackson Haines.

CHAPTER 10

Four Victorians

IT will always remain an intriguing mystery wondering whoever were the inventors of the figures eight and three, and how they were invented, whether by accident or design.

We can however trace the origin of the Counter, Rocker and Bracket.

For some years previous to Jackson Haines's visit to Europe, Englishmen were busy experimenting with new turns in an attempt to create additional figures for combined-skating, then the vogue and ideal of skating in England. During this period four men stand out. Two of them, H. E. Vandervell, the master, and Maxwell Witham, the pupil, were passionately enthusiastic about skating and from a technical standpoint they investigated their subject unceasingly for nearly sixty years. As early as 1869 they set down in print their findings by collaborating in writing the first book in any language in which the art was placed on a solid scientific basis.

Mr Vandervell began to skate about 1836, but he at once realized that before anything in the way of controlled skating could be achieved and turns executed with precision, a better skate was needed.

In 1840 he designed a model with the blade extended under the heel, fixing the whole with a foot-plate of metal. The blade now running the entire length of the boot with the heel 'rounded off' was an improvement that removed much of the danger in skating backwards with the heel but partially supported.

Mr Vandervell's improved skate was an original invention for he was quite unaware of Mr Boswell's similar skate four years previously.

Mr Vandervell, like his pupil Mr Witham, focused much of

his skating energies on the subject of turns the moment he took up skating. Firstly the inside curves, forwards and backwards, that had been in the last twenty-five years despised and neglected, were placed on the same status of importance as the outside ones. He then explored the field of 'three' turns and worked out with minute care their individual techniques, including the three changes in the figure 'Q' form. After exhausting 'Qs' and reverse 'Qs' and mastering loops and combining them with threes he continued in search of a new turn. He was following out a predetermined plan to discover every possible combination in the art of skating.

During the winter of 1860-61 he began considering the possibility of making a turn, and staying on the same edge. He began by changing direct from the inside forwards to inside backwards and *vice versa*, and from the manner he employed to execute it and the sensation it gave in the actual turning, he found the term 'rocking turn' expressed it perfectly. It is however not what we call the Rocker today, but the Counter. It was a great discovery. Hitherto when a skater made a turn, it produced a change of edge, outside to inside or inside to outside, but he remained in the same direction. This new rocking movement, in reality a counter turn, left the skater on the same edge he started with, but continuing in a different direction.

This new-found turn gave to skating much additional scope. Mr Witham discovered some years previously while skating on rollers a curious movement of making a turn in the contrary direction to turns skated in the ordinary way. Later he transplanted it to the ice. The figure commenced with a first curve of a Counter from one edge and the second curve of a Rocker from another—he named it a 'Bracket' after the mark it made upon the ice. By its nature of Counter and Rocker curves it would seem a natural sequence and known to them both simultaneously, but actually Mr Witham skated his Bracket on rollers before Mr Vandervell's rocking turn was known. In 1880 Mr Witham published in the *Field* magazine a diagram of a Bracket, and also the continuous Bracket eight. That it appeared twenty years after Mr Vandervell's invention of the rocking turn, suggests that he did not try it immediately upon the ice, believing it to be impossible to make a clean turn upon a cutting-edge. On rollers he would not have the same difficulty.

Between 1878-81 when Mr Montague Monier-Williams and his friend Mr Pidgeon were at Oxford, they experimented with Mr Vandervell's original Counter, and worked out a turn in the other direction. Pidgeon christened it the 'three-quarter turn' which was afterwards changed to 'reverse rocking turn'. When Mr Vandervell's rocking turn was later called 'counter-rocking turn', 'rocking turn' was used for the three-quarter turn which was finally named Rocker.

Although it is known that Brackets were discovered independently in Austria about the same time Mr Witham practised them on the ice, and Counters and Rockers were skated in Vienna in the late seventies, there is no doubt that the true Counter, Rocker and Bracket were first discovered and skated in England.

The discoveries and efforts of all four of the above-mentioned Victorians collected together and arranged in order formed a basis of skating technique and included the complete range of turns possible.

It is a curious fact and important, that while they were making these valuable practical contributions to skating, Jackson Haines was illustrating his idea of 'fancy skating', essentially an artistic expression of the art.

At that moment these were regarded as two distinct opposed interpretations of skating. In reality they were two halves of a whole. Although Jackson Haines practised and inspired the skating of eights and turning threes to a centre, he used them mainly as forms of exercise. He performed them in what was a revolutionary manner for the period by using the unemployed leg and arms to play a prominent part in their execution. They were a means to an end.

The rapid advancement of ice-skating throughout the latter part of the nineteenth century was entirely due to the early for-

93

mation of these two schools of thought, the scientific and the artistic. The work of these four Victorians in the formation of skating movements, their close study and creation of endless figures gave an added impetus to the improvement of the skate.

Their contribution to the development of skating was throughout scientific, and coinciding as it did with Jackson Haines's artistic expression, gave the art a solid basis to work from.

These four Victorians, particularly H. E. Vandervell, share with Jackson Haines the honour of being the fathers of modern ice-skating.

Figuring

The ability to trace the design of the figures eight and three accurately upon the ice has undoubtedly given us the terms of 'figuring', as fine skating was described in the sixties and seventies of the nineteenth century. Later, the term 'figure-skating' evolved and is now erroneously used to define the entire art of ice-skating.

Figure-skating represents only a part, the basis, although in England from 1840 onwards when skating was becoming so popular, figuring was believed to be the crowning expression of the art. The idea of marking a design upon the ice by tracing it with the skate has always fascinated skaters since the Dutch roll was known. We have seen how very early mention has been made of skaters scratching names upon the ice and in Goethe's day, a declaration of love being made. Far-fetched as some of these accounts may seem, there is no doubt that quite extraordinary efforts were made to create ambitious designs. It was this fascination that brought about the birth of pure figure-skating. After the eight and three, other numbers were attempted to be described upon the ice, such as a six and a two, and the word 'figuring' became the recognized term for such skating.

The two became a turn about 1825 but it did not bear any likeness in shape to the number. It was what we now call the 'double three' and took its name from the fact that a second three was turned on the same foot.

94

When it was found that apart from the eight and three other figures were not practicable or possible, the letters of the alphabet struck the imagination. Before there was any definite plan and recognized science in figuring one of the great delights of the skater was to invent new designs on the ice. This was particularly the case in England between 1830 and 1860, when endless ideas in shapes were attempted, and so the 'Q' figure evolved.

This figure, now no longer practised, marked upon the ice the correct tracing of the letter Q. It played an important role in the development of pure figure-skating. It was extremely simple, being a change of edge placed before or after a turn. When executed after the turn it was called a 'reverse Q'.

Mr Vandervell first saw it performed by a skater on a pond at Blackheath about 1849, and was so struck by its merits, that he lost no time in setting to work to acquire it. Soon after this he met a friend who had picked it up in a similar manner at Norwich. This confirms the way in which figuring was being practised in the middle of the last century. Wherever there was a frozen pond, a skater was figuring, after what he had seen or what he himself had invented. There was no system, nor knowledge of the existence of many of the figures then being practised elsewhere. A great variety of curious designs evolved, for, although for a long time the turns were limited to threes and the curves to changes of edges, skaters were never satisfied long in continuing to trace the same movement over and over again. The skilful skater did not care to keep to arbitrary imitations of special figures, although these were most useful for the beginner to have something to practise. Figuring was still an inventive pastime.

Advanced skaters concentrated upon the vast possibilities of the Serpentine Line. To be able to skate and alter the size of a curve, convert it into a straight line, and then again into the opposite curve to which he started, all on the same foot, was a considerable skating performance. It contained the very essence of balancing. To continue the Serpentine Line as far as possible, interpolating turns and twists with variations of outside and inside curves, forwards and backwards, was almost free skating.

Executing figures to a centre appears to have held less fascination in these early stages, mainly caused by the fact that so much importance was laid upon the marks on the ice. A figure to a centre gave less scope for design and was also monotonous to execute, being but two circles.

Figuring was for quite a time really the art of designing shapes upon the ice. When its full value was understood, it was to be transformed into a system that has become basic to ice-skating.

The Roller-skating Craze

Brief mention must now be made of the art of skating on rollers. During its first period of popularity in the seventies and eighties of the nineteenth century it played an indirect role in the development of ice-skating.

Roller-skating is an offshoot of ice-skating. Quite early in the eighteenth century a similar means of locomotion was sought which could be practised in summer. Large wooden spools attached to the shoes with strips of leather formed an early type of roller-skate, but it does not appear to have been developed beyond this stage in Holland. Yet the idea of skating in summer has intrigued ice-enthusiasts ever since skating became a popular pastime.

Garcin tried to find a way of prolonging the short ice-skating season by artificial means. He invented a skate on rollers which he called 'Cingar', an anagram of his own name, and opened a gymnasium in Paris where skaters could benefit from his invention and continue to keep up their form. Here the study of skating was practised and there is no doubt that Garcin himself discovered and improved movements with the 'Cingar' which he later tried out upon the ice. However for the majority this early attempt at skating on rollers was not a success. They found this new instrument much more difficult to control than the ice-skate, and, as accidents through bad falls were many, Garcin was obliged to close the doors.

But the idea of roller-skating persisted in the minds of ice-

25. (left) MRS THERESA WELD BLANCHARD AND NATHANIEL W. NILES. United States individual and pair-skating champions. They were founders of the magazine *Skating* and gave new life to skating in America

26. (right) ANDRÉE JOLY AND PIERRE BRUNET OF FRANCE. First great 'pair' of modern skating winners of World and European Championships and Olympic Gold Medallists

D

27. (left) SONJA HENIE. As she appeared in 1924 at the winter Olympic Games at Chamonix

28. (right) SONJA HENIE, FILM STAR AND SHOW-GIRL. She has done much to make ice-skating a popular re-creation the world over

skaters, and when J. L. Plimpton of New York designed a skate with four little wheels, another burst of enthusiasm began. The instrument was later improved, and when about 1875 the ball-bearing skate with metal castors emerged, roller-skating became the rage in Europe and America and lasted for several years. It was during this period of popularity that Maxwell Witham experimented in turns and movements on rollers and then attempted them upon the ice. Among the serious enthusiasts of ice-skating he was not alone in finding roller-skating a useful aid for keeping in form during the summer. Skaters found the attainment of skill and proficiency on roller-skates gave just as much pleasure as upon ice, but there was one drawback. Roller-skating could be practised at any time and at that period one of the charms of ice-skating was its infrequency and the doubt as to how long the ice would hold.

When the roller-skating craze was at its height, it was expected that ice-skaters would benefit from this sister art to improve their skill upon the ice. But apart from the experimenters such as Maxwell Witham, Jackson Haines and others, who definitely benefited from its practice, the general public did not appear to improve their ice-skating, regarding it more as a pastime.

Further it was considered more difficult. It was estimated then that it needed twenty hours' practice upon rollers to acquire the equivalent amount of skill which one hour's exercise on ice would produce. Therefore only very persevering ice-skaters would attempt to perform the figures they could produce on ice, and it was these skaters that found new twists and movements when roller-skating.

In England it was thought that all the ice-skating movements would be copied on the roller floor and combined-skating would be the fashion, but this latter did not 'catch on' with roller-enthusiasts. As far as roller-skating was concerned it was not only physical but social difficulties that stood in the way of its progress.

During the first outburst of enthusiasm when roller-skating was first introduced and it was a mania with everyone, the usual class barriers were thrown to the winds. The atmosphere on the roller-rink was of explosive uncontrolled enjoyment and gaiety. The sprawling and frequent falls led to the rescuing of 'maidens in distress' by strangers only too willing to lend a hand. Undesirable acquaintances were formed and Victorian parental authority took fright and put 'rinking', as it was called, out of bounds.

The ice-enthusiasts who believed their short winter season was solved by having the opportunity to practise their sport whenever they wanted were swamped by the masses of converts to 'rinking'. Money poured in at the gates and managements were not very interested in allotting special sessions for the practice of special figures by an *élite*! But the early pioneers such as Maxwell Witham were not daunted and from their practice and through their study of roller-skating they improved their own knowledge of 'figuring' for the ice.

Roller-skating very definitely at this stage helped in the technical development of ice-skating.

Combined-skating
Combined-skating was first attempted in Robert Jones's day, about 1772.

Mention has already been made in a previous chapter of an early combined-figure called the Salutation, a showy, elegant demonstration of precision and skill. No skating turn was made, but the brief approach and touching hands and return to the original position possesses all the essential ingredients required in a combined-figure.

In the first half of the nineteenth century, combined-skating became the ambition of the advanced skater in England. All efforts to find new turns and movements were inspired by the possibility of being able to use them when skating in concert with others.

As early as 1831 simple turns in the form of threes were introduced and by the middle of the century combined-skating was considered in England as the highest expression of skating art.

Its principal appeal was the pleasing effect it produced when executed by a number of skilled skaters. The team spirit so necessary to its success had also its fascination. The English play best when working as a team, and in a way combined-skating was a game in which the object was to unite the various figures in a combination of movements.

At first there was no rule as to numbers, any convenient number could join in providing they were able to execute the figures and movements agreed upon. It began as a technical game, and was to develop into an exacting art. In these early stages teams formed and the building up of many diverse combinations resulted. Perfect timing was essential and the inter-weaving of figures and circles without collisions when skilfully done gave a pleasing effect.

The Skating Club of London can be considered the first society to have put 'combined figure skating' upon a planned basis. It began with simple movements and very quickly possessed a repertoire of five figures which were practised regularly by the club members. As the art developed and new turns were discovered, the best skaters introduced them into their exercises and combined-skating became a performance of considerable skill.

To carry out a figure successfully it was not sufficient to be just a good skater, for each taking part had to be equally matched in ability with the others as to power and control.

Any number of between two and nine skaters could take part. Four was considered the best number, able to carry out the most complicated movements in the repertoire, but six and eight often managed the ordinary movements without difficulty.

A general centre was taken by placing a wooden ball upon the ice, upon which the skaters converged. Later an orange became the recognized centre, for it could be seen easily and rolled over the ice better than the ball, without danger of tripping a skater should he foul it.

One skater was selected as captain or leader, whose duty it was to call out in a clear voice on approaching the centre the movement he required to be skated. This was termed 'calling'.

99

After advanced skaters had executed the repertoire of official combinations set down by their various clubs, they would go on to carry out new movements at random. It was here that the success of a figure depended a good deal upon the caller, for the whole movement was under his control. He required a thorough knowledge of the different movements and an ability to combine them in such a way as to ensure continual variety without violent transitions. Perfect timing was needed when making the call and also careful judgement in the selection of the figures to be skated, for carried out in this way combination-skating had all the elements of a game.

A figure was begun by the skaters standing opposite each other on four sides of a square. The first pair started together, followed immediately afterwards by the second pair, all four doing the same movements. The second pair's retarded start was necessary to avoid collision, so the first pair could first clear the orange. Should odd numbers be taking part, then the odd man would cut in after all the others. It can be seen at once that this position needed excellent judgement and was filled by the best skater.

When as many as six or eight skaters were taking part, the first pair would be about to complete a figure as the last pair were starting. The effect to the onlooker who did not understand the plan was one of confusion and so later a Mr W. C. Marshall introduced a new idea whereby all the pairs would start off simultaneously, skating the same movements at the same time. To avoid collision at the central pivot, no crossing was done, and an imaginary circle was drawn around the true centre about two feet from it. As the skaters approached the orange they ended their movement or turned upon the outer circle, which produced a very charming effect of opening and closing like the petals of a flower.

Combined figure-skating of this nature united in the performer all the qualities of pure figure-skating, complete repertoire of movements, precision, balance and control. To the onlooker it was a fascinating spectacle to witness.

Combined figure-skating was never seriously attempted by a

skater until he had acquired considerable skill in executing the complete repertoire of pure skating figures individually. Skating with others held a strong appeal to the Victorians. Its technical requirements were both stimulating and fascinating; interest never flagged and figure after figure could be exercised. For them it was the most delightful of outdoor pastimes and could be continued for long hours.

Combined figure-skating was the symmetrical execution of a figure by one or more pairs of skaters. Symmetry was the essential and demanded three indispensable factors—the figure had to be skated the same size, on the same lines and at the same pace. If any one of these requirements was missing, then it was not a true combined-figure. The prime test of such skating was that at any moment the skaters forming each pair should be found executing the same movement at equidistant points from the orange, and opposite to each other, so that a line drawn between them would pass through the centre.

Combined figure-skating was the 'acid test' for the skater's skill. Through its severe demands upon symmetry it emphasized at a very early stage the technical growth of skating proper and stressed its essential properties.

CHAPTER 11

English-style Skating

ARTISTIC skating received its first impetus in England in the eighteenth century, in its primitive form. It was exaggerated, for gestures were overdone and posing was indulged in to excess. When a century later the technical development of skating figures was taking shape, and it was thought that this latter form of skating was the direction in which the art should follow, the original and wider interpretation of skating like a dancer was neglected in England.

At the commencement of the Victorian era it was completely abandoned and indeed attacked as a shocking display of immorality. Little wonder then that Jackson Haines with his theatricalism had no success when he visited England, where, during this long period, skating degenerated as a true art form but made gigantic strides in technique.

The tremendous enthusiasm for figuring, the discoveries of new turns and movements, and the practice of combination-skating demanded a special study of these technical elements. The art became a science, and it was practised as such.

The artistry of motion as meant by beautiful action was removed from skating and a cold science substituted. Pleasure was condemned in the execution of the figures and combinations, which were to be performed in a restrained and dignified manner, and the only enjoyment experienced was a feeling of pride in their accurate execution.

Victorian austerity imprinted itself deeply upon ice-skating and a special style synchronizing perfectly with the tone of the period evolved. It came to be known as the 'English style' and for a long period was the only form of skating practised by the authoritarian members of the Skating Club. But its true designation should have been 'Victorian' for it echoed both in manner of performance and in dress, the moral tone of the era.

Top hats, black frock-coats and trousers, as worn by the Skating Club members, allowed of no frivolity in figuring.

A 'static' conception of skating resulted. A rigidity of the back, with the arms and unemployed leg held stiffly to the side of the body, was an altogether unnatural manner of travelling across the ice; ease and grace, two of the essential elements in skating were missing, and by not using the free leg, turns had to be done by a sharp flick, another unnatural movement. This stiff and ungainly style of skating persisted and flourished throughout the Victorian era in striking contrast to the graceful and expressive style of the Continent. This latter, with the free leg and arms employed to the full expressively, and the rhythmic sway in turning was regarded by the Victorians as unmanly, affected and even immoral.

This austere approach of these English skaters precisely figuring upon the ice, resembled a squad of soldiers performing some old-fashioned ceremonial drill. It is a curious paradox therefore that this so-called English style which advanced an unnatural theory of skating should discover and further so much the technical development of the art.

It can be explained by the fact that concentration on the absolute necessity of 'doing it properly', led to a profound study of figuring that discovered the technical secrets of twisting and turning. When this was known, accuracy was possible. The complete understanding of the figures invented and the radical improvements of the skates required to perform them were the concrete results and invaluable contributions the English style made to skating. It was a mixture of pure technique and sport. Music, an imperative adjunct to skating, was then non-existent, and yet this 'artless' form lingered on till late in the thirties of the twentieth century.

The Viennese School

During the period between 1870 and 1890 when the English

skaters were inventing and elaborating turns and twists for their combination-skating, another school of thought was forming in Vienna.

We have already seen the deep impression Jackson Haines made upon Viennese skating society during his lengthy stay in the capital. His conception of skating was beautiful and thrilling. It was an art. The Viennese loved it, believed in Haines, and adopted his ideas.

When he left Vienna around 1870 he left behind him talented pupils, who became the nucleus of a new approach as opposed to the then fast-developing English conception. Both systems were to prosper for sixty years or so, before finally the Viennese conception was to triumph.

Vienna in the last century was a very gay city. It was waltzing-mad to the intoxicating tunes of Waldteufel, Gungl and Strauss. And to the Viennese, skating could not do without music. Military bands became a regular part of the Viennese skating scene, and inspiring marches set the skaters off on their rollicking spree. This of course was the lighter side of skating in Vienna, but it was this natural gaiety and *joie de vivre* upon the ice that was instrumental in fashioning the future direction of the Viennese school.

It must be remembered that Jackson Haines brilliantly illustrated this conception of skating, but he was a lone artist, a very personal one, and who had been regarded in his own country of America and in England as an exhibitionist or stunt-skater.

At that time the English method was being practised extensively by the serious skater on the Continent. English skaters were already exhibiting their ability in many of the capitals of Europe and reliable literature on the subject was limited to English authors, whose works were translated at an early date into German and Swedish.

And yet Vienna soon became a centre of skating thought with the Vienna Skating Club, which was formed in 1867. The result was the Viennese school of skating, completely different, in an atmosphere of pleasure and gaiety, where dancing and music dominated.

Dr Gilbert Fuchs, the first World Champion who skated the classic figures with power and gusto, and Gustav Hügel, his successor to the title, who introduced in a brilliant fashion fascinating dance steps into his free programmes, were the first outstanding exponents to illustrate in competition this Viennese conception.

The large ice surface of the club situated near the centre of the town was not merely a frozen surface for members to practise upon, but nightly became a pleasure-ground. Carnivals and fancy-dress balls were staged and these gay revelries, lit by electric and Bengal lights, were often watched by as many as 3,000 spectators. Ice-skating was becoming a spectacle, and not only an exercise or recreation.

Differences of the Two Styles

The Viennese school and the English style of skating were so completely in contrast to one another, as to purpose and manner of execution, that it is small wonder that sooner or later one or the other style would triumph over its rival. It is interesting to note that at this stage the English style technically was very much in advance of the Viennese school. This was mainly due to the exacting demands of combination-skating. But with all the progress English-style skating was making as a science, its purpose was limited, for combination-skating was plainly a technical pastime governed by exacting rules that restricted development once perfection in skill had been obtained. Naturally, endless combinations of turns could be invented, and in fact this is exactly how the advanced skater in England satisfied his skating ambitions.

The Viennese school by its love for theatrical display and musical interpretation possessed unlimited possibilities for the development of skating since its purpose was to make it an art.

To the Viennese, skating meant primarily something to see, to the English it was something to do.

In execution the two styles were in direct contrast. The stiff ungainly method of the English skater was made necessary by the precise demands of combination-skating. The unemployed leg remained inactive. The arms with their elbows turned in, were slightly bent or hung loosely beside the body. Such stance had to be strictly observed for any wild swing of the leg might lead to a collision or would throw the neat design out of place. But the main reason for these rules was to produce a uniform style, for the keynote of combination-skating was uniformity, for a good effect could only be obtained when the different performers skated in a similar fashion.

An inclination of the body suggesting grace was not in keeping with the ideals of combination-skating which attempted fine control and approached this ideal in the manner of a game. For skaters who possessed considerable skill and indulged in skating in consort frequently, it afforded considerable pleasure as a pastime, for the strict rules and the constant variation of patterns that were possible, made combination-skating an excellent exercise in control. The manner in which it was performed however was absolutely contrary to the natural deportment of a skater, but all the figures could be skated with the least appearance of effort to onlookers.

The Viennese school built its theory upon the presentation of symmetry in deportment. Even a complicated movement upon the ice meant nothing in itself if the carriage of the body was awkward or ungraceful. The skater's arms and legs were therefore used to the full. The rigid back was relaxed, the skating leg could be bent, the free leg poised elegantly behind and the arms gracefully placed outstretched above the waist. The style was free and unrestrained and therefore made possible true artistry in movement. The skater was allowed full liberty of action in the execution of figures. The result was a graceful harmonious effect.

The employment of the arms and free leg in the turns at this stage of development was at times haphazard. The lack of a standard method for controlling the swing of the arms and the

106

carrying of the free leg led to a great diversity of undisciplined movements. But the principal effort was concentrated upon beauty of movement, which is what skating should be.

The Viennese skater some time before the birth of the Viennese school knew from the translated work of Cyclos variations of threes and double threes and independently discovered a Bracket, and when the Counter and Rockers were known practised all these figures in the Viennese manner. Swinging the arms and legs to help these turns before these figures were properly understood led to changes of edges and 'kicking' turns.

The English skater at this stage had the technical advantage over his Viennese rival of being equally skilled upon both feet, an absolute requirement of the English style.

Actually Viennese skaters were executing 'bastard' turns, as the English termed them, late into the nineties of the last century. This however did not hold up the general advance of the Viennese school, whose artistry and musicality was in full development.

CHAPTER 12

Special Figures

BETWEEN 1870 and 1890 ice-skating had become a very popular recreation in winter over the greater part of Europe and on the North American continent. But it was only in England that a uniform system was practised. No new movements were accepted unless they were in keeping with the aim and development of combination-skating.

In Vienna, across the Continent, and in Scandinavia, spread a wave of enthusiasm for grace and elegance, and also for movements that thrilled, such as spinning, 'spread-eagling' and jumping. These performances formed a category apart from the skating of basic figures, such as eights, threes and 'Qs', and were termed 'special figures'. They became a part of skating proper when in competitions in the early 1880s, skaters were given the opportunity of showing their proficiency and brilliance in unusual special figures on the ice.

There were numerous variations of these special figures created by master skaters, including a certain number from the American continent, particularly Canada, which were characterized by their complete novelty.

The loop was one of these original figures. It was then performed in a straight line and repeated as many times as the performer could continue without breaking down. A rather drunken effect was created but later, when it was discovered the skater could control the movement, long designs were made across the ice and the one who made the greatest number of loops on one skate was considered the best exponent of this figure. From this spinning loop evolved the Ringlet which differed only in that, instead of being merely circular, it was perfectly round. Performing Ringlets in a straight line was much more difficult than loops, and not many could be done at one time, but performing Ringlets was fascinating and a double Ringlet was tried out. The skater after executing one, circled a second time over the original tracing of the Ringlet and then skated out of the circle after which the figure ended. When it was discovered it was easier to perform a loop in its place, Ringlets went out of fashion. These circular movements performed in a confined space and of symmetrical design were the beginning of another type of skating of which we will read in another chapter.

From the loops evolved the Anvil, a figure which for many years was to play an important part in skating but finally was destined to fade completely away. It originated in Canada about 1870 and took its name from its outline upon the ice. Later the figure was known as the 'cross-cut'. It was discovered through the failure in the correct execution of a loop.

Beginners today when learning loops frequently fail to get a perfect round curve, and produce a small straight cut at the apex of the loop. This is because the body is not in proper balance with the foot, the latter arriving at the top of the loop before the body, which causes a slight slowing up in the movement, when the skate slides back a fraction waiting for the body to catch up and swing round, the skate naturally follows it and the loop is made. However by encouraging this tendency of the skate to stop and slide in a straight line, the cut made at the culminating point of the loop could be made with certainty, and of considerable length. This was a cross-cut. The entire movement was done on the outside edge. Several variations were invented and, in spite of their difficulty, were to enjoy much popularity among advanced skaters for many years before they went out of fashion.

The Compass circle was another novelty from Canada. The free foot was 'riveted' to the ice by the skate-point while the skater circled around it with the other foot, making several circles, the number depending upon his skill. These variations, forwards and backwards, with changes of edge were called 'toe-circling'. No movements performed on skates so closely resemble perpetual motion. They were the forerunners of the pivot movements, which modernized have become part of classical skating today. Grape-vines, of which there were many variations and which have already been mentioned in a previous chapter, originated in Canada also.

The New World liking for the sensational was one reason for the early development of such original skating movements just described. They were unique in that they departed entirely from the general direction skating appeared to be pursuing then.

Although many New World skaters practised the English style, others who had visited Europe, came back convinced that the Viennese manner was, if not the right way, anyhow the most pleasurable manner of skating.

The considerable interest in special figures in Europe and North America between 1865 and 1890 brought in a new phase in skating development. But it was only the 'adolescence' of a maturing art.

Continuous and Fancy Skating
During the same period between 1870 and 1890 when 'special figures' were in full development another form of skating was evolving. The feat of being able to perform a series of special figures upon one foot without allowing the free foot to touch the ice was known as 'continuous skating' and was then considered the most difficult form of skating, for much agility was required. This style was widely practised on the Continent and in Scandinavia, where high degrees of skill were achieved by star performers.

Continuous skating originated in a very limited form more than a century before when Robert Jones described the efforts of skaters to continue the Serpentine Line as long as possible. This changing of edge in a straight line performed on one foot and repeated several times led to the new development in which impetus was gained by the change of edge and the swinging of the unemployed leg.

Nearly every figure in the existing repertoire could be skated

110

by skilled exponents. But the high light of continuous skating was the invention and execution of figures which first displayed ingenious designs upon the ice, and yet also demanded considerable skill in their execution.

The leading skaters were able to cut accurate and complicated designs representing anything from a pair of spectacles, or oxhorns, to a double shamrock or Maltese Cross. There was no limit to invention in this special branch by the star skaters of Russia, Sweden, Austria and Finland. For a while it was to occupy an important place in the international competitions.

It was also popular on the American continent, particularly in Canada. In England it was little practised, the main reason being that continuous skating was impossible without a bent knee, swinging leg, or arms in free movement, all these points being regarded as 'bad form' in Victorian skating circles.

'Fancy skating' was mainly an offspring of continuous skating with the essential difference that the figures executed were in a form more artistic than the well balanced and precise mathematical designs of the latter. They were not valuable contributions to skating proper, rather demonstrations of a skater's skill. The reason for their existence lay in the challenge of being able to depict upon the ice objects such as a rattlesnake, fishes, leaves, letters of the alphabet and numerals. As the skater's skill developed and his ambitions grew, so the variety of design became greater. The manner in which they were executed was of little importance so long as the finished outlines were successful. Therefore, correct body position and elegance, essential points for skating a figure, were more often than not forgotten. Most of the designs were performed upon one foot, but two-footed patterns were also drawn.

George Meagher, a Canadian skater who won many trophies from various skating clubs in America including an open competition in 1891 in Ottawa that laid claim to the World Championship,[2] was the most graceful exponent of fancy skating. He

[2] First official World Championship 1896.

invented and performed a large repertoire of such movements.

But perhaps the very summit of ingenuity in this direction was the ability of the American skater, Dr Barrin, to cut one of his initials with one foot and the other initial with the other at the same time. In the later stages of the nineteenth century fancy skating was especially popular on the American continent where the taste for stunting was always revelled in.

'Fancy skating' was often wrongly applied in describing the performance of spins, jumps and spirals, but these figures in the early stages belonged in the category of special figures, a group which comprised true skating movements.

Women and Hand-in-hand Skating
Ice-skating is the only sport in the world that has a patron saint, St Ludwina (or Liedwi), who had the unfortunate accident referred to in a previous chapter.

From the earliest times when ice-skating was first taken up in Holland, women delighted in being escorted over the ice by their men—they created a pretty picture on the ice and inspired many a painter to portray the skating scene. But from skating as a recreation women ventured on to the frozen canals, and when travelling from village to village even rivalled the men in the Dutch roll, and in the sixteenth century they first took part in organized speed races. The experience required for these performances by the hardy Dutch women was born of necessity—they were country folk whose quickest and best way to market was along the lengthy stretches of frozen canal.

But as true ice-skating as an artistic pastime developed, women did not participate in anything like the same measure as men. In fact for more than a century most were content to delight in simpler enjoyments in a comfortable sleigh that was either dragged over the ice by a horse or pushed by their admirers. Marie Antoinette was one of the first women to show a real liking for artistic skating proper.

It was in England however where women were first offered the opportunity to vie with male skaters. Combination-skating inspired 'hand-in-hand skating', devised for their mutual enjoyment.

As early as 1836, the pioneering Oxford Skating Society possessed a simple programme of 'club figures' for hand-in-hand skating. As in combination-skating it needed a modest proficiency in essential figures, and the ability to skate backwards.

The danger of falling was really the main obstacle that prevented ladies taking up skating. First it was difficult to convince women that the terrors of falling would not be fatal. Afterwards when the Empress Eugénie, Queen Victoria and the Empress Elizabeth of Austria ventured on the ice, this fallacy was destroyed, but an equally frightening idea developed in the fair sex's imagination. To be seen falling was far more terrible than the fall itself.

But they really never needed to worry about their first hesitant steps upon the ice for there were always several cavaliers at hand only too delighted to have a companion to initiate into the joys of skating.

The manner of holding hands was of great importance in this new branch of skating. There was one fashion where partners held each other with one hand only, the other being permanently disengaged. This was called the 'link' method, but was not considered very nice to see and the majority of the united figures were performed with the skaters clasping both hands.

There were three ways of doing this. The first, face to face, partners looking in opposite directions, the man taking the lady's left hand with his right, and *vice versa*. The second position, the skaters were side by side, shoulder to shoulder, both facing in the same direction, the man taking the lady's right hand with his right, passing it behind the lady's left in front of her, and taking her left with his. The third manner, was one behind the other, the man being behind the lady, both facing in the same direction, the man taking the lady's right hand with his right, and her left with his. This way of holding hands was known as the Austrian method but was rarely practised in England. There was also a variation of this called 'Echelon', partners holding both hands,

113

right in right, and left in left, facing the same way, the lady slightly in front of the gentleman.

Hand-in-hand skating derived from combination-skating and so the figures attempted and executed did not depart from the basic figures then practised in the classic style. There was however an endeavour to break into a freer and speedier expression of movement and there were a few figures known as 'progressive united figures' that suggested modern ice-skating. These figures were termed 'scuds' and as the expression implies, skimming across the ice at speed was the main joy and object of the movement.

The Mercury scud was the oldest of the hand-in-hand figures and when partners were able to skate well together a great speed could be obtained. The skaters held hands facing one another and the movement was cross-rolling forwards and backwards, so that when one was skating the cross-roll forwards, the other was doing it backwards. The cross-rolling was alternated from side to side so that the skaters could travel across the ice in a Serpentine.

This early figure in hand-in-hand skating exercised in a methodical manner contributed considerably to the advancement of skating. Skating together, hand in hand, had been practised as far back as the seventeenth century in Holland where Dutch rolling along the canals and over the frozen stretches of the Zuider Zee, was a common sight. It was well done in unison, and was the very earliest type of pair-skating. But it never went further than that, and although it naturally gave delight to both performers, it was basically a means of crossing the ice from one point to another; whereas the Mercury scud used an individual movement of skating for two skaters together to be executed with method and style to produce enjoyment in its performance and an aesthetic effect for the onlooker. It therefore possessed purpose and meaning.

There was the 'Q' and 'back scud' which was a pleasant figure to skate and attractive to look at. Both skaters performed the same movements, a forward 'Q' followed by a back, one skater making 'Qs' always on the right foot and the other always on the left, one partner preparing to make the change of the 'Q', while the other skated the cross-roll from the 'Q' on the back. When the skaters grasped each other's right and left hands alternately, changing hands each time one of the skaters commenced his or her 'Q', a very pleasing effect was obtained.

There were a number of these progressive face-to-face scuds, based on the classic individual figures, of which the 'Q' form was very popular. Forward and back Rocker scuds were more difficult and were for the advanced hand-in-hand skater.

The non-progressive united figures consisted of the various simple figures skated hand-in-hand without scudding. They were called non-progressive because none of them could be skated without pausing before beginning the figure on the other foot. Furthermore before beginning the figure, the skaters had to get up a certain speed by straightforward skating.

The simple figures skated in this manner consisted of all the forward turns and the forward 'Qs' and reverse 'Qs'. The advanced skater attempted Rockers with success.

In the non-progressive figures an important element for the future development of hand-in-hand skating evolved. It was not understood immediately, but was later found to be the correct method for obtaining the best results. It came about because the man was the stronger skater and so he always led. As hand-in-hand skating became more popular, a proficient method was devised to soften the break at the finish of a non-progressive figure and attempt a graceful change-over before the start of the figure on the other foot.

Shortly after a turn had been made, the lady would gently pull nearer her partner, whereby her speed was increased and his retarded, hands were then set free, as she passed the gentleman well in front of him. Hands were then joined again, and the partners were now in position to start the preliminary straightforward run for the figure on the other foot.

A harmonious action for the passing from one figure to another was evolved. It was pleasant to do and to look at, and

115

simply inspired the idea for further combinations of hand-in-hand skating.

Towards the end of the nineteenth century this form of skating had become so popular that there was the danger of abandoning individual figures and skating alone.

Hand-in-hand skating differed from combination-skating in that the latter aimed primarily at the perfectness of the figure, whereas the former laid its emphasis upon the aesthetic effect of harmonious movement together. It was the beginning of pair-skating.

PART THREE
THE HEROIC ERA

CHAPTER 13

The Growth of Skating Clubs

THE first firm basis of ice-skating was made in the nineteenth century when skating clubs mushroomed in many countries in both Europe and America. They were the means of establishing a method and general understanding of skating essentials.

During the period of discovery and rapid development of so many skating theories between 1830 and 1890, clubs were the medium that collected this immensely varied matter and stored it in their archives for the benefit of their members. Without this enthusiastic organization many learners would have strayed, and the development of the art been retarded.

We have already read about the founding of the first skating club in the world, in Scotland sometime during the early part of the eighteenth century. At this early period the main object of the Edinburgh club was 'to enable members to skate together in consort', which required, as the club notices stipulated, good attitude, correct timing, close contact of partners and an ease in movement. Method, the Edinburgh club insisted, was one of the primary functions of the existence of the club.

It was not until 1830 that the Skating Club was founded in London, in the same year as the Glasgow Skating Club. A full description of the former and its very important role played in the development of skating can be found in an earlier chapter. As for the Scottish club, it has inscribed its name indelibly in the story of skating through its President, George Anderson, who under the name of 'Cyclos' wrote the first serious book upon the subject.

This club was also the first in Great Britain to depart from the stiff Victorian style in skating. About 1875 officers from the

100th regiment who had been stationed in Canada, introduced a 'small tricky style of skating'.[3] It was then not looked upon by the English clubs as 'good form', in fact was considered by them as a set-back in skating development.

The invention of an improved skate-iron by Mr Henry Boswell, an Oxford citizen, was the main reason for the founding of the Oxford Skating Society in 1838. This club, benefiting from this improved design, created a school of skating of its own, which appears to have been in advance of what was then generally known in figure-skating.

The United States was the next to follow England and Scotland and founded the first club on the American continent in Philadelphia in 1849. This club played an important role in the popularizing of skating in America, and was instrumental in giving the impetus to other cities to form clubs. The skaters of the Delaware and the Schuylkill frequently visited New York and they were responsible for grouping together the many skaters living in the city, which resulted in the foundation of America's second club, the New York Skating Club in 1863.

The same year saw the founding of the Christiania Skating Club in Norway and a year later a number of Englishmen living in St Petersburg founded the Neva Skating Association to be known later as the St Petersburg Skating Club, which for many years was to have among its members some of the finest skaters of the day.

In 1865 the Marquis de Morny with three other noblemen formed the *Cercle des Patineurs*, who met on the frozen surfaces of the Bois de Boulogne.

At this period clubs were being formed in many of the larger European cities, and Vienna founded the Vienna Skating Club in 1867, Troppau followed in 1868, Budapest and Copenhagen in 1869.

In 1871 the Wimbledon Skating Club was formed outside London and during the seventies, eighties and nineties this club played an important part in popularizing skating among the

[3] This is according to Monier-Williams, see p. 8. (Introduction) in his book *Figure Skating*.

general public. It was a centre for learning the rudiments of artistic skating, although hundreds could never hope to join the club itself, for the standard was high and membership difficult to obtain, because of a very severe test that every lady and gentleman had to pass before acquiring the coveted badge of membership.

Between 1880 and 1900 innumerable clubs sprang up in England and skating knowledge expanded considerably.

The Foundation of the National Skating Association

From 1870 onwards skating in England was developing rapidly, and it was felt among the leading skaters of the day that an authoritative body to govern the destinies of the sport should be formed.

The Skating Club in London with its many expert members had filled this role admirably for more than three decades, but it was essentially a club, and its opinions and manner of skating could not be forced upon other clubs if they did not wish it.

The creation of a union grouping among its members the most enthusiastic and knowledgeable skaters of the day with the purpose to promote figure-skating as well as steer its destinies in the right channels was encouraged in 1879 by the foundation of the National Skating Association of Great Britain for the promotion of speed-skating.

This branch of ice-skating was very popular in the Fen country and before the nineteenth century began, championships took place regularly on Whittlesea Mere and elsewhere. For that area with its long stretches of frozen ice was one of the best places in England for skating and Whittlesea Mere in particular became a centre of the sport.

The local competitions, championships and frequent record-breaking of classic distances brought speed-skating in at a great pace, and it was this branch of the sport that was instrumental in the founding of the first skating union in the world.

The National Skating Association of Great Britain was founded in 1879 to promote speed-skating, but its creation was

121

caused more by an anxiety to protect this great new popular sport that had gripped hundreds of enthusiasts throughout the country.

Wherever there was enough ice, races were organized and handsome cash prizes were offered. Amateurs joined in with self-styled professionals, and betting and sweepstakes were the order of the day. All classes took part and it was not an unusual sight to see a black-tailed parson scorching down the fen in a straight-mile contest, encouraged by the enthusiastic crowds and parishioners massed along the ice.

Money rewards and punting inspired irregular practices in some contests that each year appeared to become more frequent and threatened to destroy the original high ideals of the sport.

On 1st February 1879 a number of true sportsmen associated with ice-skating, headed by Mr James Drake Digby held a meeting at the Guildhall, Cambridge, to discuss ways and means of stopping these all too frequent practices and enforcing the correct conduct of the sport. That day saw the birth of the National Skating Association, and a month later, the Duke of Devonshire, the Earl of Leicester and Mr C. W. Townley, the Lord Lieutenant of Cambridge, were invited to be presidents. When a few weeks later the first general meeting was held with Mr Townley presiding, the scope and objects of the association were clearly defined.

Two years later figure-skating was added to that of speed-skating in its operations. The secretary, J. D. Digby, to whom most credit must go for the setting on foot of the association, at once appealed to figure-skaters generally to help him in organizing the figure-skating division. He was very fortunate in being able to mobilize from the very beginning the aid of H. E. Vandervell and Monier-Williams. The former was the first great name in modern scientific skating, the latter a young follower who later, as we have already read, completed the final chapter in basic systematic skating.

The principal aim the NSA had in view was to popularize figure-skating by creating three graduated tests of merit, for

122

which distinctive badges were awarded for each examination successfully passed. Any skater in England could join the NSA by paying a small subscription and so automatically qualified for the tests.

No better idea could have been invented for the improvement of scientific skating which at this period was the only pure form of the art of skating. But the reward of badges for the successful passing of such tests shocked many skaters of late Victorian England. Quite a lot of the skating world, among them a number of first-rate performers, were against the NSA and kept away from it because they thought the introduction of tests with badges as compensation, was violating the pure amateur status of the art. It must be remembered that in England where skating had developed quicker than anywhere else as a scientific *art*, it was practised as a *sport*, yet was in fact one of the few sports in the country 'untainted by professionalism and betting in any shape or form'.

These Victorians had a horror that their sport might develop into a vulgar game where competition was the sole object. They practised it as a distinguished exercise of skill and elegance where science harmonized with beauty of movement. They were, in the Victorian manner, executing a graceful art that did not need the introduction of competition to inspire it.

Although the reward of badges for the tests successfully passed was of no intrinsic value, the idea might grow into compensating skaters with money prizes if a craze for competition in figure-skating developed. The early members of the NSA were not against the idea of competition within certain limits, but they were undoubtedly against money prizes and sporting contests on a large scale such as a British championship.

Figure-skating as practised in England at this period had no professionalism in it, and the popular practice of betting that was applied in many sports, was never allowed to intrude in any shape or form. However these tests helped enormously in the development of better skating, and even where no club had yet sprung up, and communal inspiration was non-existent, the solitary skater upon a lonely pond became enthusiastic about the science, because of the existence of these tests. Now that a standard had been set by the NSA, skaters were stimulated to master the principles of the art, and travel many miles to present themselves before the judges.

When towards the turn of the century artificial ice-rinks came into being, giving added facilities to the figure-skater, the NSA introduced a further test, called the 'special test', considerably more difficult than the first class, evidence that tests were good for the improvement in skating, and had been accepted as such.

The First Competition

The first competitions in ice-skating were speed contests. Speed inspired rivalry and the velocity that could be obtained in skating was far greater than what man could reach by simple running. Speed thrilled, and it can be assumed that in the early days after the invention of the iron skate, running matches of sorts took place in various parts of Scandinavia between local rivals. But it was in Holland during the sixteenth century where speed-skating contests had reached a high level in organization and a certain brilliance in performance. There were both men's and women's races; competitive skating had now become a sport and a regular feature in the winter life in Holland.

Although artistic skating was practised in Holland at the same time, it was limited to the Dutch roll and attempts to cut names upon the ice. It was a means of locomotion and a pastime, and the latter had no definite rules or planned direction to follow.

Two centuries later Benjamin West, the American artist, is credited with being the first man to win an artistic-skating championship in the 1770s. Although there are no records as to where it took place, it is quite feasible to believe that it was in London. Skating in England was in full development at that period, the time of Robert Jones, and West who was President of the Royal Academy had already gained a reputation as a fine skater.

124

But artistic skating had not developed sufficiently to allow it to be taken seriously for competition purposes when compared with speed-skating.

Speed contests became the dominating feature of ice-sports in Holland and by the middle of the nineteenth century could be considered the national sport. Big prize money, as much as 250 *gulden*, was offered to the winner in the towns, and in the smallest of the villages the fastest skater could pocket between ten and fifty *gulden* in an afternoon. The runners were mainly market men whose daily work in winter led them over the frozen canals, and they were practised in fast skating. The 'gentlemen' figured principally as judges and spectators. There were even races between teams made up of a male and female skater linked as a pair.

But it was in Denmark just after the middle of the nineteenth century when the title of 'artistic skating competition' was billed in conjunction with speed contests; but after the usual series of speed races for men and women, which included a race backwards of more than a mile, the artistic part of the programme terminated the competition and took the form of an obstacle race. To negotiate the twelve stumbling-blocks placed upon the ice at various intervals was undoubtedly considered an art, and neither a game, nor mere race!

But artistic skating in competition on the lines of a modern championship had its roots in Vienna. With the legacy left by Jackson Haines, skating along artistic lines was developing fast and in the 1870s several competitions took place which included figure and free figure movements. An international speed and artistic-skating competition took place in the winter of 1871-72 when the best skaters from Northern Germany competed against the Viennese. There was a ladies' competition in 1875 and in January 1879 the men's competition, staged at night under the new fascination of electric lamps, gave a great impetus to the competitive side of artistic skating.

Certainly other cities in other countries staged similar though smaller contests whose records have been lost. Champions were beginning to be born, some were self-styled or rather self-crowned after an easy victory in an unofficial competition organized for the benefit of showing the winner's skill over all comers. There were too some very fine skaters who were recognized as national skating champions, but competitions in which they claimed their title were not yet seriously organized.

In 1882 an international skating contest was held in Vienna, at which were represented many of the countries of Europe. Leopold Frey, a Viennese and pupil of Jackson Haines, won this competition. Edward Engelmann, also of Vienna, came second and Axel Paulsen, the Norwegian, whose skating jump has become world-famous, finished third.

This competition can well be considered the first real artistic-skating competition for two reasons. First, the winner was an implicit believer and follower of his teacher's methods. In carnivals he appeared in costumes copied from his master's; but Leopold Frey not only carried his master's art before the judges but convinced them and the onlookers that day that skating on this model was an art to develop.

Secondly, Leopold Frey competed against fine skaters, some of the best of the day. This meant that ice-skating had arrived at a point where skaters were keen to challenge and not only to exhibit. Artistic skating had found a new and intriguing means for development, in competitive skating.

CHAPTER 14

Special Figures and Free Skating

I T was during this first big international competition in Vienna in 1882 that a very important decision was made concerning the direction of the development of skating art.

The special-figures section which afforded the competitors the opportunity of showing their proficiency and brilliance in movements other than the basic figures, produced on this occasion a mixture of free-skating combinations and figure designs.

Headed by the winner, Leopold Frey, the majority of competitors followed the true idea of skating art and presented a number of elegant movements joined together to make a whole, a special figure as it was then called.

Leopold Frey linked an outside Spread Eagle to a back outside eight and terminated on a Jackson Haines sitting pirouette.

Axel Paulsen performed only one movement in presenting an outside forward three jump with one and a half revolutions landing on the left backward outside. This jump was to become the most famous jump in the free-skating vocabulary. Heinrich Jokl used the Grape-vine, linking it with a loop and a three.

All these were skating movements, pieces of free skating.

But Theodor Langer presented in this section a filigree design of a four-point star. It was a figure design upon the ice, an advanced idea of continuous skating, skated throughout upon one foot; and although it needed the basic skating figure of change of edge, forwards and backwards linked with cross-cuts, the figure had to be performed in such a jerky fashion with the skater's eyes glued upon the ground, and his body often in an ungainly position, that it was opposed entirely to the idea of skating art. It was anti-skating, yet the drawing left upon the ice was greatly attractive, symmetry being very near perfect.

To perform such a figure was highly unspectacular. It was the age-old idea of trying to cut one's name upon the ice in uninterrupted skating on one foot, brought to a very high level.

The presentation of this type of skating by Langer put the judges in somewhat of a quandary.

The design drawn upon the ice by him was unquestionably attractive, but the manner in which it was created was not skating art. Furthermore, it was impossible to determine the superiority of a figure like this with real free-skating combinations, when there was no common measure of comparison.

Nevertheless the judges gave the first three places to exponents of free-skating movements although the brilliance of Langer's four-pointed star left an indelible impression on them, the public and particularly the skaters competing.

Its execution needed a fine control over skate and body and the successful performing of such a figure demonstrated a considerable skill on the part of the skater.

The finest skaters of the day accepted this new vogue in figure designs and a new branch of skating developed. In competition it took the title of 'special figures' and the real skating movements came to be known officially as 'free skating'. Both were treated as separate categories later.

After Langer's star design they were often alluded to as 'star figures', because a great number of the imaginative creations were worked out on star patterns. The correct designation should be 'figure designs'.

For quite a long period in the nineties and at the beginning of the twentieth century this branch of skating was placed in the forefront of skating artistry, and halted the development of pure skating. More than anything else it was a skater's ability to cut upon the ice the most original creation in artistic design and to execute it with ease and elegance that stamped him as a champion.

But the craze for designing was a temporary diversion from the true course of development in skating. It did however show how much could be done upon a skate.

29. CECILIA COLLEDGE. British Ladies' Champion who caused a
sensation by closely challenging Sonja Henie in the winter Olympic
Games of 1936. She won the world title in the following year

30. DAVOS ICE STADIUM. Supplementary rinks at the side enable all the different ice sports to be practised simultaneously. It is a rendezvous for every great name in all branches of skating

The Russian Scene

Mention has already been made of the early creation of a skating club in Russia, the Neva Skating Association, whose foundation in the winter of 1863-4 was due to the initiative of enthusiastic English skaters living in St Petersburg. From it the St Petersburg Skating Club was formed which in the nineties produced some of the finest skaters of the day and some of the most dazzling spectacles.

The club through its foremost members developed to a high degree the new category of special figures, and they were predominantly successful in this branch.

They inherited from the first English members of the club the idea of the importance of symmetry in drawing the basic figures upon the ice, and so these special figures inspired the artistic side of the Russian skater to combine skill with creative imagination. Design upon the ice was of greater importance than skating performance.

It was in Russia and Russian Finland where the most numerous and many of the most important competitions in this branch were held. This idea of skating became a real craze in Russia and competitions to encourage the invention of new figures were specially organized. In 1909 their importance in Russia was so high that one competition excluded the compulsory skating of the basic figures in favour of these figure designs, and the programme was completed with free skating.

Russia at this time boasted some of the pre-eminent skaters of the day and St Petersburg was a centre for some of the earliest big international competitions.

Another influence which had an important bearing upon skating habits emanated from the St Petersburg Club. It was the becoming skating attire worn by the ladies of the Neva club. High boots and a tunic with the collar and borders embroidered with fur and an attractive fur cap. The men adopted a similar style and for more than fifty years this mode of attire was favoured by skaters throughout the world.

Every year the Neva was the scene of a dazzling carnival or-

E

ganized by the club. The Czar and members of the Imperial family came to see it and skated. The ice-field was bordered by coloured lights and in the centre was an enormous snow figure from which shone a brilliant illumination like a lighthouse. Many of the skaters carried little coloured lights on their caps and in their belts and as they skated round in the dark, they looked like giant glow-worms. Cannons fired large snowballs that burst above the rink and sprayed the skaters like confetti. These fêtes upon the Neva were the most extravagant and luxurious carnivals of the time. The Russian skating scene during this interesting period just before and after the beginning of the century was generally characterized by extravagance. If at times the ideas appeared somewhat fanciful, they were always visionary, and contributed a great deal to skating in this development stage.

The International Skating Union
With the formation of skating clubs that were springing up in many centres in Europe and on the American continent definite ideas and rules were forming fast, but these independent bodies were impressing their own personal imprint upon the art and its direction, resulting in national and international differences.

When the first skating association in the world was founded in England, a significant resolution was made at the first general meeting, to promote the establishment of international skating contests in various countries under the direction of an international council. Here was the seed that thirteen years later gave birth to the International Skating Congress, held in Scheveningen, Holland, in 1892. It was attended by six countries. Austria, Germany, Great Britain, Holland, Hungary and Sweden. The congress lasted three days from 23rd July to the 25th and gave a great impetus to skating as a sport.

In the following winter of 1892-3 the first amateur championship of the world in speed-skating took place at Amsterdam. To gain the title needed an athlete of astonishing power and brilliance. The competition consisted of four distances, viz. 500,

1,500, 5,000 and 10,000 metres, and in order to have the honour of being called Champion of the World it was necessary to win three out of four races. It meant the champion had to be a sprinter, middle- and long-distance skater.

Jaap Eden of Holland won the first three races and so was the first official skating champion of the world.

In 1896 the International Skating Union held its first championships. It was then called Championship of the International Skating Union but as its entry list included the majority of the leading skaters of the day, it was regarded as the World Championship and since the International Skating Union is the international body that is qualified to organize world events, 1896, date of the ISU first championship, marks the era of official world competition in figure-skating.

The establishment of the International Skating Union confirmed the world-wide interests in skating activities. Its formation made skating a world sport.

CHAPTER 15

Skating in the Alps

SWITZERLAND being a mountainous country of snow and glacier it would be natural to imagine that a primitive form of locomotion over snow and ice had been invented there in early times, but apart from the *luge*, the Alpine form of a sleigh, no other means of winter transport had been evolved. Both skis and skates were imported to the Alps.

The abrupt Alpine slopes covered thick and heavy with snow appeared too steep and dangerous in winter. The small routes and paths sufficed for means of communication between the villages and the mountain lakes that froze would always be skirted by a land path. Winters in the inhabited parts of the Alps never lasted longer than three months. The *luge*, pushed by man, pulled by a horse or propelled by its own momentum down a steep road, filled all the requirements of the mountain Swiss in winter time.

Skating in the Alps had been practised at the end of the sixties in Davos on a sheet of ice situated in the garden beside the *Kurhaus*. A group of male skaters danced the quadrille. They were a mixed gathering of Dutch, Germans and Russians. They had been attracted to Davos for health purposes—Alpine air, the glorious winter scenery and sunshine being considered a cure for bad nerves and general worries.

Skating on the part of visitors in the *Kurhaus* garden was very probably impromptu; they wished to have some fun and to put some life into the new resort.

But skating in Switzerland began seriously in the Engadine during the seventies, when a band of English enthusiasts who had spent the previous summer in the Alps, taking the waters at St Moritz spa, suggested the idea of returning there in winter

132

time to put in a few weeks of skating. Heavy frosts in England appeared to be more and more rare, and sometimes a skating season melted down to two or three days. The big lake before St Moritz lay free and beckoning. The idea was excellent but a hardy one, for the journey was long and tiring, and the hotel in St Moritz that opened for them specially was not equipped for winter residence.

From Chur the travellers had to hire a coach and ride along the route the Romans took over the high Julier Pass. Heavy snows blocked the way and a blizzard howled at 8,000 feet, taking them three weeks to arrive at their destination.

Next morning, with spades and brooms they cleared a small corner of the frozen lake from snow and in the afternoon were skating on the natural ice of St Moritz.

The English skater had discovered a new part of the world where ice-conditions were very favourable and where skating could be exercised more or less regularly for a period of three or four months. For the English enthusiast with means and time to spare, such an opportunity was not to be lost and very shortly skaters from England began to come out every winter to this part of Switzerland. These visitors inspired the luxury hotel in the mountains and it was in Davos where skating took on a real importance in the winter. In 1875, the Hotel Belvedere was opened and at once filled with English skating enthusiasts, and so became a hotel exclusively for pleasure and sport in contrast to the other establishments whose guests were mainly in Davos for their health.

It was the English guests at the Belvedere that planned the first ice-rink in Davos. A number of Englishmen found the patch of ice in the village that the locals slithered over not large enough, and so a group of these visitors planned with the manager of the hotel to construct a rink. The exigent demands of the skaters for good ice laid the foundation of a tradition that has been kept up till modern times. This ice-rink opened in 1877 was not for the exclusive use of the English skaters, for all nationalities were welcome; nevertheless the practice of the

133

'Victorian style' of combination-skating occupied such a large space and the English being in superior numbers and better skaters dominated it, and it became known as the English rink.

A rival rink was opened later to accommodate the German and Russian skaters. This lack of space at such an early stage in the development of skating in the Alps made a deep impression upon Davosian authorities, and this is one reason why rinks in this resort have always been on a giant scale.

On the so-called English rink, a number of health-seeking visitors established another custom that was to grow with the years and become a part of the life in Davos in winter time. When the weather was fine and sunny they sat around the rink watching and enjoying the gyrations of the skaters.

At the same time as the English skaters were planning the first rink, another Englishman suggested the foundation of a club. The original idea was for it to be an English club for English skaters only. But when the initiator of the project approached the local authorities and put before them his plan, they pointed out their disappointment that it did not include the other visitors to Davos. The English had skating in their heads, the authorities had Davos in their hearts. It resulted in the formation of the first Davos Skating Club in 1880, with a large membership of 200, of many nationalities. In 1881 a rink nearly double the size of the first was opened and called the rink of the Davos Skating Club. A large porch covering the entire north side of the rink was built affording a protection to skaters from the bitter north-east wind that frequently blew. Seats for spectators lined the borders and in the hall a buffet was installed for refreshment. Nearly every afternoon music played for the benefit of the skaters, who hailed from as far afield as America and India. It was the first international rendezvous in skating, and in 1894 the International Skating Club of Davos was founded.

It was an important step for skating, for it gave the opportunity for skaters from every country to meet and exchange ideas regularly at a centre where skating thought was in full development.

The success of Davos as a winter resort with its luxury hotel crowded out with winter sportsmen was soon to have a great rival in St Moritz where the luxury hotel was later to dominate the village and make it the most elegant winter resort in Europe. Each big hotel had its own rink and this later made St Moritz a great training centre for top-class competition skaters, for with as many as thirteen rinks to choose from, training could be carried on in comparative secrecy.

St Moritz and Davos became the pivotal point in the Alps for skating—capitals of the skating world.

Skating in Scandinavia

Axel Paulsen of Norway was the first great Scandinavian skater, although skating had been indulged in for centuries in Northern Europe. He practised both speed-and artistic skating and contributed much to both these categories. In collaboration with Carl Werner, another skater from Oslo, he constructed a racing-skate of two thin metal tubes, a blade one sixteenth of an inch wide, and no doubt inspired by the Jackson Haines figure-skate; the narrow metal plates were screwed to the boot. It was a complete departure from all skates used for racing till then. Its lightness and more secure fastening were the chief advantages over previous designs and this tubular system has served till today as a model—the modern hockey-skate is the outcome of Axel Paulsen's speed-skate. After outstanding performances against his rivals in Norway he visited the United States, Canada, England, Germany and Holland in search of fresh laurels and it was his influence at these contests that brought about the early international competitions in speed. Mention has already been made of the jump he presented in the international competition in Vienna in 1882, which has perpetuated his memory in skating.

In Sweden racing was popular too, but after Jackson Haines went to live in Stockholm, artistic skating experienced a great boom under his inspiration, and by the end of the eighties this form of skating had become the national sport of the country. In 1889 a contest in figures and free skating in Stockholm drew a

135

crowd of more than 20,000 people round the rink. On this occasion a team from England had been invited to give an exhibition in combination-skating. It was not the style or the idea of skating practised by the Swedes, but the Stockholm Skating Club was a cradle of experiment in the eighties and nineties, and it was uncertain then whether this type of skating would be taken up as a sport or not. Their clean-cut controlled figures and emphasis upon precision in figuring impressed the Swedes and was to become a hallmark of Stockholm skating after this.

Competition in artistic skating was encouraged very early in Sweden, and junior school championships were numerous. This produced many promising youngsters who later were to influence the development of artistic skating, particularly in England.

The second World Championship for men took place in Stockholm and was marked by the appearance of Ulrich Salchow, the vigorous Swede whose name was from then on to echo forcibly throughout the skating world. He gained second place in this contest and afterwards won the World Championship ten times, the European Championship nine times, was the winner of the first Olympic skating competition and collected thirty-eight Gold Medals. Both these individual triumphs as examples and his personal efforts gave a tremendous impetus to the art in his native country. Sweden became, after Vienna, the second great influence in skating.

Salchow's almost perfect school figures, acquired through careful study and practice, and his conception of a free-skating programme of well-spaced movements were followed by the Swedish school of skating.

Working on these lines, the Swedish school was to produce a number of outstanding performers during the following twenty-five years. Treating it as a sporting art, making it less theatrical and more accurate in execution, that was the Swedish approach.

Touring
There was another form of skating that enjoyed great popularity in many countries during this period. 'Touring' on skates over

136

large stretches of frozen fen or lake or—better still—over Dutch canals, was thought by many to be the greatest fun in skating.

It did not demand such exacting athletic qualities and high physical condition that speed-skating needed. Touring could be practised by all, and had the added element of adventure in it.

The great lakes of America with their seas of ice, hundreds of miles in extent, were fine fields for touring, but there was always the danger of violent gales or blizzards overtaking a party some miles out, which rendered their position dangerous. New Yorkers used the Hudson and made long trips up to Albany.

The fjords of South-west Norway and the lakes in Sweden below Stockholm that extend to the Baltic were popular touring areas, the scenery and splendid setting tempting many English enthusiasts to abandon their business preoccupations for a few days' tour in Scandinavia.

Heavy snow-falls in Canada and Northern Europe were frequent and so rendered touring uncertain over long periods.

In England the Fen districts of Norfolk, Cambridgeshire and Lincolnshire were fine touring grounds as long as a heavy frost lasted. 'Fen-running' as it was termed also had the element of risk in exploration. Ice, owing to the treacherous rivers, was not always firm and a knowledge of conditions and the necessary equipment was essential if any ambitious programmes were to be attempted.

A strong heavy stick or 'bandy' was used for feeling one's way on doubtful ice, the method being to strike it hard to see if it would bear. A strong cord of about twenty yards and two mince pies were recommended by experts to complete essential equipment. The first two items were necessary, for 'duckings' were quite frequent. In good winters, tours of sixty and seventy miles could be made in one day and almost without traversing the same ice.

But it was in Holland, the country of still shallow waters with its large network of canals where touring was ideal. This was the branch of skating that all Dutchmen practised and in winter in Friesland when the frozen highways were thus in use, trams

137

and trains ran nearly empty. Every town and nearly every village and individual house could be reached on skates.

The canals were kept clear after a heavy fall of snow by sweepers, who were paid by the municipal authorities, or, in some cases, by local skating clubs. Everything possible was done during a frost for the encouragement and enjoyment of skating. Every few miles along the canals at important places and in the villages and towns, stalls were erected for warming refreshment with a kettle of hot spiced milk always ready on the boil. When evening came and the canals were deserted, bands of sweepers would brush the ice with long brooms, sweeping away the wear and tear of the day's skating. Hot water was used to fill up the bad cracks when it was freezing hard, and planks and straw were laid down over really bad patches. Tufts of reeds were placed at dangerous spots to warn the skater, and guide-posts on the principal canals were placed to direct him.

From Amsterdam tours were made in all directions, to Haarlem, to the Zuider Zee, to the island of Marken with its 'ice fair'. But it was in the Friesland, the land of Holland's most enthusiastic skating tourists, a national pastime, and the ambition of the best 'tourers' was to visit in one day the eleven cities of Friesland on skates. This was a circuit of 120 miles or so, over canals and lakes and through woods, and needed considerable training before an attempt could be made. Climatic conditions had to be excellent, safe ice, no snow, no wind and a full moon to light the way for a very early start.

Each skater carried a sheet of paper that he got signed by an inhabitant of each town, proof that he had passed by. The average time taken was between sixteen to eighteen hours and when completed was written up in the daily press and recognized as a great skating feat.

Three Englishmen accomplished the circuit in fourteen hours, a record that stood for some time, but was later lowered to just under thirteen hours by a Dutch skater. The attempt to beat this last record transformed somewhat the real idea of touring into racing on this route.

This form of skating had much to recommend it in Holland, where the conditions were ideal for it, but it did not contribute anything towards the development of skating. However it helped, by its character, to develop the love of speed-skating, a domain in which Dutch skaters still play an important role in international competitions today.

CHAPTER 16

The Establishment of Artificial Ice-rinks

DURING the nineties a new element gave a great impetus to the development of every kind of skating, establishing itself in the form of artificial ice palaces.

Experiments to produce real ice by artificial means received encouragement in the seventies when skating in an artistic form began to be understood. In comparison to speed and touring, a very small space was needed. To acquire skill, much practice was required, and climatic conditions in a country like England where skating was developing fast, were far from ideal. In America, at approximately the same time, enterprising promoters were making projects and designing buildings for skating rinks, but they never got beyond the experimental stage.

The first artificial ice-rink in London was Mr John Gamgee's small room in a back street in Chelsea. Sometime earlier he had built a small ice floor of twenty-four feet long by sixteen feet wide, protected by a canvas-covered tent. But the first real rink, off King's Road, Chelsea, was in a permanent building with an ice floor forty feet long by twenty-four feet wide. This was in the winter of 1876. Mr John Gamgee's patented process of refrigeration was used. There was a gallery for spectators where on occasions an orchestra played for the benefit of the skaters. A noted artist from Paris was brought over to decorate the walls with Swiss Alpine scenery. The rink was not open to the public, but noblemen and gentlemen subscribed.

This exclusive rink was much talked about and other promoters speculated on building rinks for popular entertainment. Rinks of a certain size were constructed at Manchester and Southport, the former closing down after about twelve months. Southport which opened two years later in 1879 struggled on for ten years before it was obliged to close through lack of support.

During this early stage excessive dampness and thick impenetrable mist pervaded these experimental ice-rinks and was the principal reason why their life was short. Skaters found them unhealthy places.

But in the nineties real improvements were made, and good ice in comfortable conditions was now possible.

The big capitals, London, Paris and New York, each had two rinks, and Brighton, Brussels, Munich, Philadelphia, Baltimore and Brooklyn one each.

All these ice palaces were at first much frequented, for they were something new in entertainment, and the general public invaded them when the craze began. But this raised a problem for the serious skater, for crowded rinks gave him little chance to practise his figures. This was the main reason why the Princes Skating Club in London came into being. It was a long hall in Knightsbridge with a sheet of ice 200 feet long and fifty feet wide, and exclusively for the use of members, the public not being admitted. Here at Princes, the *élite* of English skaters went through their paces.

Apart from this idea of a private club where the enthusiastic support of serious skaters made the running of the hall a financial possibility, the public rinks ran the risk of having to shut their doors after a few years' existence. The general public soon tired of skating round and round in a limited area, and so the rinks began to empty. The restricted figure skating enthusiasts were not enough to turn the rinks into paying concerns. Yet somehow they remained open, often aided by private financial support, and played an important role in popularizing skating in general. Ice-hockey matches were played, and the third World Championship for men was staged in London at the National Skating Palace, known as Hengler's, as early as 1898. These events took place under the protection of a roof, free from the uncertainties of the weather, which was a marked improvement on conditions for the skater.

Artificial rinks made skating possible in countries where it

141

could never have been otherwise introduced owing to the general climatic conditions.

The first rink in Australia opened in 1904 in Adelaide, and a year later the Melbourne Glaciarum was built and since its official opening in June 1906 has not missed one season. It was the cradle of skating in the southern hemisphere. A year later a rink was opened in Sydney and in 1909 another was built in Johannesburg, South Africa.

The same year the first open-air artificial ice-rink in the world was opened in Vienna by Edward Engelmann, an engineer and former European Skating Champion. This was an epoch-making date in skating for the success of the Engelmann rink set the fashion in Central Europe for this style of arena.

The name of Engelmann is a household word among Viennese skaters. Edward Engelmann's father, himself a skating enthusiast, used to take his young son to see the exhibitions of Jackson Haines. In 1867 he installed a small surface of ice in the courtyard of the factory he managed in Vienna. This was the modest beginning of the Engelmann Sport Arena. At first it was only for his skating friends and family, but a few years later it blossomed forth into a successful commercial enterprise.

Edward Engelmann junior, became Austria's first European Champion, winning in 1892 and 1894. With the increasing popularity of skating among the Viennese and the unstable weather conditions that prevailed in winter, he set about to remedy the situation and began to study the problem of artificial refrigeration in the open air. Helped by the great experience of his father and a group of friends his project became a reality in October 1909. It was an instant success, and a second open-air artificial rink was opened in 1912 on the land of the *Wiener Eislauf Verein* with the vast surface of more than 10,000 square yards. A third open-air artificial rink was opened in Vienna just before the outbreak of World War I. Hungary was the first country to follow Vienna's example, then Prague, and much later Switzerland.

142

The artificial ice-rink was an important contribution to all branches of skating, for it spread it throughout the world.

Invitation to the Waltz

When Jackson Haines was delighting Vienna with his brilliant exhibitions of skating in the sixties, the 'uncrowned king' of that gay city was the waltz, and the Viennese skaters danced on ice.

There is, however, no substantial evidence that the waltz on ice originated there. What is certain is that the introduction of ice-dancing proper owes much to the Vienna school of skating. Skating in pairs to music was what the Viennese enjoyed and they certainly made many attempts to transport the most popular dance of the nineteenth century on to ice. This resulted in a certain number of 'two-footed' ice waltzes being attempted. More often than not, both feet were touching the ice together and resembling the floor waltz in the length of step. Their originators approached their task by trying to copy rather than adapt, for these two-footed dances were but attempts to reproduce the floor waltz, and were not suitable for long glides over the ice. A technique for basic skating steps had to be employed if a dance on ice was to be successful.

The English with their enthusiasm for the technical side of skating attempted to waltz on ice in England around 1880, and in the international atmosphere of St Moritz and Davos some English skaters tried to discover suitable steps for a waltz on ice, and there is strong evidence that one of these skaters later in Canada hit upon the idea of using the simple figure three, and, stretching far back the free leg, danced the first ice-waltz in Halifax, Nova Scotia, in 1885.

The first official performance of the waltz was in Paris at the *Palais de Glace* in 1894 by Monsieur Richard, the skating instructor there. Its success was immediate and after seeing it English teachers of skating took the dance back with them in 1895, to the Niagara and Hengler rinks in London. There it was an instantaneous success. Never had a new idea in skating attracted and conquered so quickly. It became the goal of the rink novice.

But in spite of this the combination-skater and his partner unrestrainedly expressed their dislike and disgust at 'dancing on skates'. It was a new-fangled 'Continental' idea that was injurious to the dignity of the sport. It lowered the tone of combination-skating, which was a noble science executed with dignity. Nevertheless these dignified exponents passed remarks at the waltzing couples, and some even deliberately obstructed them while dancing on the rink.

On the Continent, however, the vogue spread like wildfire where it was danced in a very light fashion. This simple three-step waltz brought in a new branch of artistic skating, proper ballroom dancing on ice.

On with the Dance

With the invention of the ice-waltz, dancing on ice in a modern sense was established. Its immediate and overwhelming popularity was an indication that ice-dancing had a brilliant future.

Enterprising and inventive skaters soon imagined the delightful variety of floor dances translated to the ice. This was to come later, much later, but in the meantime a skating dance was invented.

The 'ten step' has no counterpart in the ballroom; it is essentially a dance on ice and came into being through such an approach—its dash and speed are essentially ice characteristics.

The actual date of its invention is rather obscure, for with its exhilarating and captivating tempo it seems to have 'arrived' in several places at more or less the same time, though Vienna seems entitled to the biggest proportion of honour. One of her skaters, Franz Schöller, may be credited as being the composer, or at least having exercised most influence upon it at the time of its inception. For quite a while it was known under the name of *Schöller-Schritt* and contained just ten steps. About 1907 the first four steps were repeated with a short outside roll on the fourth step, making the dance fourteen steps, and at the same time giving to it its final name.

It quickly spread all over the world and was often danced in

31. (left) MAXI HERBER AND ERNST BAIER. Several times European and World Champions and Olympic Gold Medallists in 1936. This German couple was one of the finest combinations ever in pair-skating

32. THE AUTHOR AND HIS WIFE IN THEIR WELL-KNOWN SHOW NUMBER *La Belle Époque*. They pioneered modern ice-dancing in Switzerland and so far have been the only Swiss representatives in this branch of skating in the World Championships

33. (right) KARL
SHÄFER IN A STAG
JUMP. Finest product
of the great Viennese
school, whose fine
performances in
European and World
competition gave a
new impetus to
skating popularity

34. BARBARA ANN SCOTT IN A STAG JUMP. The little Canadian
girl in one season won all possible major championships. In
1948 she was Canadian, North American, European and World
Champion and an Olympic Gold Medallist

35. HANS GERSCHWILER. Swiss champion and World Champion in 1947

36. JEANNETTE ALTWEGG. This British champion has claims to being the greatest school figure skater yet. She won European and World Championships and was the Olympic Ladies' Skating Gold Medallist in 1952

its early stages to waltz time. Its construction corresponds completely with the natural requirements of skating. It is a skater's dance.

The Triumph of the Continental Style

Curiously enough there never were two styles in ice-skating. In England during the time of Robert Jones when skating there was practised as an art and developing fast, the English skater was an elegant and graceful performer. His Serpentine Line, Salutation, Spread Eagle and figure of a heart were executed with poise and an attempt at beauty of movement. It was a style, and interpretation of skating. Primitive though it was, the manner of expression was the corner-stone of the art. It has been referred to as the original 'Old English' style. It owes this title to the fact that English skaters in the middle of the eighteenth century were the only ones truly attempting to develop ice-skating.

Beauty of movement in gliding over the ice and elegant pose during the execution was the only style for artistic skating, although during the nineteenth century the English skater 'froze' to a poker-like rigidity. As the slightest demonstration of theatrical pose on the part of the skater was regarded as 'bad form', a ramrod artificiality took its place. This we have seen was called the 'English style'. This unartistic manner of skating developed the scientific combined-skating, apex of the Victorian skater's ambition.

There were of course a few English skaters who admired the so-called 'Continental style'. Some practised it and believed in it. Edgar Syers was one, and he brought over to London two brilliant Swedes, Ulrich Salchow and Henning Grenander, as fine exponents of the Continental style, to show English skaters, as he himself put it, 'what the Continental style was really like'.

The power and grace with which they performed their programmes, and particularly their ease in the execution of classic figures effected a large conversion. From then on artistic skating in England was assured.

The staging of one of the first World Championships in

London in 1898 was due to the energy and persistence of Edgar Syers, in the face of considerable opposition and finally derision on the part of the Victorian skater. Mockery was the only weapon left to the English-style skater who refused to be converted.

The transformation was fairly rapid when it is considered how firmly entrenched was the English style. It was of course continued by the die-hards, but the youthful newcomer embraced the Continental style, and so every year increasing numbers of English skaters practised artistic skating.

The English had always called it the Continental style, to distinguish the manner in which other countries of Europe skated in contrast to themselves. On the Continent and in America it was known as the 'international style', because of the many countries adopting it. It really should have been called the 'natural style', at the time when the Victorian skater was attempting to force his petrifying theories of 'form' upon the skating world, and the revival of the natural art of skating in England was an important feature for artistic skating.

CHAPTER 17

The Role of Women in Skating

EVER since the early form of artistic skating began in Holland with the Dutch roll in the seventeenth century, women have practised it. They partnered their male companions in gliding over the ice, and it was principally for charming company in a novel pastime that they were tempted to skate.

There were a few, such as the Princess of Orange, who learnt to skate and perform artistic movements by herself. But in the eighteenth century the demonstration of artistic skating was a masculine practice.

In the middle of the nineteenth century when scientific skating was developing fast in England, the lady skater began to take an active interest in this science of figuring. It was through combination- (combined-) skating that the English lady skater in the seventies and early eighties became proficient in skating. But even then, though she practised the art seriously, her position was still like a fourth at bridge, a partner to fill in the gap.

Nevertheless on the Continent where natural artistic skating was advancing, it was becoming quite clear that skating was peculiarly suited for feminine practice. Enthusiastically they entered the field of individual skating, and very soon boldly challenged the men in official competition when Miss A. Malmgren of St Petersburg competed against some of the finest men skaters of the day in an international competition held in 1890 in the Russian capital.

Male superiority in skating was shaken violently in the men's World Championship held in London in 1902 when Mrs Madge Syers of England was placed second to Ulrich Salchow, the champion.

Madge Syers and her husband were the foremost converts to

the international style, and several years previous to its recognition and establishment in England they were known on the Continent as distinguished performers of it. Madge Syers herself developed into a brilliant exponent and as the International Skating Union had not instituted a ladies' championship, there was only one resource—to compete against the men.

It was a World Championship and so open to all skaters, distinction of sex not existing, and it was never expected a lady would dare to enter.

In this championship Madge Syers skated so well that many believed she should have won. As runner-up to the great Ulrich Salchow she set the skating world talking. By her triumph she hastened official recognition of women's role in skating and brought about the early institution of a ladies' World Championship in 1906, which was skated in Davos. She won it, beating Jenny Herz of Austria, the young lady who also made history by being the first female performer of the Jackson Haines 'sit-spin'.

1906 was the date in which a new phase of artistic skating came into being. Women working in their own independent field were to enlarge the possibilities of this developing art. Now being able to rival in skill and performance the men, a further advancement in skating evolution was possible. Pair-skating could now be developed to a high degree, and so by their collaboration they made it possible to develop and complete the finest expression of skating art.

Skating in America

Although as early as 1886 American clubs had united to form the National Amateur Skating Association of the United States, and national championships for men had been organized before that, and were still held yearly, skating developed very slowly there. Public interest was entirely lacking and these so-called National Championships drew more contestants than spectators. Two days were sometimes needed for one competitor to complete his figures. He and everybody else was obviously very tired after it all, and such competitions gave no stimulus to skating art.

148

Philadelphia, the cradle of the sport in the United States was practically the only centre of interest, but even here only twenty to thirty persons practised artistic skating.

Then Irving Brokaw of New York went to Europe to study and practise, and returned to demonstrate its fine qualities. He wrote a very comprehensive textbook explaining all the movements. He himself at the time was the best exponent in America and like Edgar Syers in England a decade before, never tired in his efforts to introduce along the eastern seaboard the style and ideas that were being established in Europe. Interest was slowly aroused and in 1913 the Skating Club of Boston brought over from Germany a professional skater to teach the art of figure-skating. Through Brokaw's continuous efforts, an international fancy-skating tournament for the United States Championship, with competition open to the world, was staged in New Haven, Connecticut, in 1914.

'Fancy skating' was an out-of-date term wrongly used for figure-skating. It merely emphasizes that the elegant art of skating was far from being established there. The ladies' category was won by Theresa Weld of the United States and the men's event went to Norman Scott of Canada, who partnering another Canadian, Jeanne Chealier, carried off the pairs.

The First World War silenced the new sport just at the moment when it might have gained a little more popularity after the competition mentioned above, which appeared to have made a certain impression. But figure-skating went into eclipse and remained so for a few years.

But a new idea was to help considerably in keeping alive an interest in artistic skating. It was also an importation from Europe, the professional ice-show. Certainly it was the American Jackson Haines, who inspired them, for the first carnivals on ice in Vienna, St Petersburg, Troppau and Munich and elsewhere in the eighties and nineties of the last century were the result of his showing the real meaning of beauty of movement on skates for interpreting music, and adding to this a theatrical costume.

When in the first years of this century artistic skating was be-

149

coming an internationally organized sport, competition in the form of championships was slowly taking the first place in the interest of the serious skater from the great carnivals and fêtes on ice that were once the annual high lights of the skating season.

But in 1908 a permanent ice-ballet company was conceived in Berlin. Between fifteen to eighteen professional skaters were employed and for nearly four seasons they played to an enthusiastic and increasing skating public at the *Eis Palast*. In the season of 1912-13 at the *Admiral Palast*, a company of nearly thirty skaters very successfully performed a sort of musical comedy on ice, entitled *Flirting at St Moritz*. Then the outbreak of the First World War cut short the professional ice-show in Europe.

Irving Brokaw's love of skating was not limited to amateur figure-skating, and it was his suggestion that these German skating ballets then being performed in Berlin would go down well in America. In 1915 the management of America's largest playhouse, the New York Hippodrome, imported the stars of the Berlin ballet and forty of the most talented and beautiful girl skaters and introduced ice-skating entertainment to the United States with an American version of *Flirting at St Moritz*. It was a sensation in entertainment for the New York public. Although the frozen stage was small, the performers were able to show off the long flowing curves of skating together with clever and intriguing footwork. Amateur competitions were also staged there and over 3,000,000 people saw these professional and amateur exhibitions. Further, to encourage its development, booklets illustrating the methods of the star professionals were distributed to the audience.

The success of this theatrical entertainment brought about the vogue of cabarets on ice, and many of the big hotels followed the example of the Sherman Hotel in Chicago which constructed in 1914 a miniature ice-rink in the dining-room. Some were built on roof-gardens and terraces in many of the capital cities.

The establishment of theatrical entertainment in skating was a new phase in its development, an angle which later was to contribute considerably to its evolution as an art.

150

Another stimulant to skating running parallel with this new form of spectacle was the arrival in America of Sweden's foremost teacher, Bror Meyer. His pedagogy and his theories helped to form the basis from which the modern American school was to spring.

The First Theatrical Star Skater

It was again Jackson Haines who became the first professional show-skater, when he gave exhibitions on rollers at the Alhambra in London, and the first star when he roller-skated the skating ballet in the opera of *Le Prophète*.

The first professional ballets staged in Berlin before the First World War created a new type of performer, the 'theatrical' skater. The stars were principally girls—who did much to help in the spreading of skating ideas.

The leading skater of the Berlin ballet who was brought over with the company to perform in the old New York Hippodrome was Charlotte Oelschlagel, who became the first theatrical star in ice-skating shows. She had fine theatre sense and remarkable skating skill for that time and nightly she thrilled an audience of 6,000, during a run of more than 300 days, an American theatre record at that time. Before long she was billed on Broadway in blazing letters simply as 'Charlotte'. Smothered in a white fluffy costume that just covered the knee she electrified the packed Hippodrome public with a theatrical performance of skilful skating. She was the first woman to include an Axel Paulsen jump in her routine programme which she terminated with the famous fade-away ending, which she created. She was always experimenting with new ideas and her performances had the brilliance and freshness of something great about them. She was a Broadway star and it was as the queen of show-girls that she became 'the toast of New York'. The greatest enthusiasm ever seen over any theatrical entertainment in New York followed Charlotte's skating exhibitions at the Hippodrome. She was acclaimed by many critics as the greatest skater in the world. A 'Charlotte Waltz' was composed for her and in 1915 she became the first ice-

151

skating star in the cinema. She played in a serial 'photoplay' in six parts entitled *The Frozen Warning* and the plot was of the spy variety so popular in the nickelodeon period, with Charlotte as the heroine. In the first ice-skating scene presented to the public on the movies, Charlotte, who discovers the plot, warns the hero at a skating-rink party by skating the word 'spies' on the ice.

She was described in the publicity posters as 'the Greatest, most Graceful and Wonderful Ice Skater in the World in a Photoplay of Great Appeal'.

She herself had great appeal and was undoubtedly the most spectacular exponent of ice-skating of the time. She was under twenty years of age when she first starred in New York and this fact was something unusual for the period, for many considered her as the world champion. Through her skating skill Charlotte became a theatrical star and it was as a 'show-girl' that Broadway idolized her.

Charlotte had firmly established the art of ice-skating in 'showland'. Theatrical skating was now to become a permanent feature in the art, the skater being an artist more than a sportsman.

CHAPTER 18

The Importance of Competitions

JUST previous to the outbreak of the First World War artistic skating in Europe had acquired a large vocabulary of movements in figuring and free, and a coherent understanding of the correct way to employ them had now been worked out, and international competitions were to be the stimulus and peak for ambitious skaters.

In 1901 the Scandinavians organized the Northern Games in Stockholm, rallying seven countries to compete in speed- and figure-skating. 1908 was a memorable year, for pair-skating was officially given a place in skating art by the International Skating Union, and the first World Championship in pairs took place in St Petersburg. The same year at the Princes Skating Club in London, the first Olympic skating competition was organized.

From this year onward international skating championships for world titles in all three categories were held annually in different skating countries of Europe, the ladies' and pair-skating now being on the same level as the men's.

English skaters were adopting in ever-increasing numbers the international or natural style of skating, and England had already become one of the leading countries in it. Together with Sweden, Austria, Hungary and Germany, they dominated the competitive skating scene prior to 1914.

After the hostilities, competition was soon established again and in 1920 the newly opened rink in Antwerp was the stage for the second Olympic skating competition. Although some very fine exponents of artistic skating from the North American continent had competed in some of the very early competitions in Europe previous to 1890, this Olympic contest was the first time the United States officially sent a skating team to represent it in Europe. Theresa Weld and Nathaniel W. Niles of Boston, two of America's best skaters, were selected. Another outstanding feature of this competition was the arrival of another great Swede, who was to leave a strong imprint upon skating in the 1920s. Gillis Grafström, an architect by profession, skated to his first Olympic victory in Antwerp. He gave to his skating a particular light beauty in execution that had a touch of mystery about it. It was his own personal manner of expressing himself upon skates. Apart from this, he broke away from the traditional method of Salchow, that was the classic basis upon which international skating had been modelled. Grafström gave more freedom in execution as well as in interpretation. He brought a kind of poetry into skating, approaching it purely as an art and not a sport. He also developed skating by creating combinations of spins and jumps among which are included the 'flying sit-spin' and the 'change-foot spin'.

International competitions became the 'trying-out ground' of new developments in skating. New ideas in movement and combinations were approved or condemned by the critics, and the chance to be selected for the championships was the aim of every skater with ambition.

In 1924 in the winter Olympic Games at Chamonix a new factor was born in the evolution of the sport. A small child of eleven years old staggered the austere company of adult competitors by entering for the ladies' event. She represented Norway and her name was Sonja Henie. She was placed last but by what she did and the way she did it, she created a new era in skating. Extreme youth was in the van—Sonja Henie suggested the future. She was the future personified.

Fours

At this time an unusual branch of skating was practised in North America. It was called 'fours' and had its place in important competitions in the United States and Canada.

It was an offshoot of the former English combined-skating. This latter branch had been practised in both countries for some time before the final conversion to the international style.

Fours, differing from the original idea of school figures being performed by a group in unison, were made up of two pairs executing a variety of free-skating movements and combining them to a pre-recognized plan and performed to the accompaniment of music. It was a kind of skating ballet. Any of the individual or pair movements such as spirals, spins and jumps could be adapted in a four programme. As in English combined-skating, a leader was chosen to call the moves, but this was only while the moves were practised. For exhibitions and contests, the programme was unprompted.

The four skaters often commenced by converging from each corner of the rink and meeting in the centre to face one another, then, like an invitation to the waltz, they started in pairs, separated for a few simple three turns, joined for a moment, separated again and pirouetted to complete the opening pose. The substance of the programme was filled with spins, jumps, spirals, Spread Eagles and stepping. Pair-dancing was preferably avoided in the formation of these programmes as it tended to emphasize differences in speed and style which resulted in the couples performing independently and straying in extreme corners of the rink, the illusion of the four being entirely lost.

This conception of artistic skating demanded a constant returning to the pivotal point around which the programme was constructed. It was not necessary to be in the middle of the rink, but the centre chosen was a focusing point of the main scenes, as it were, for both the spectators and the judges. For competition purposes the demonstration had to be judged as a four, therefore the compact execution of the various movements was a necessity.

One of the important features of this type of skating was its team-work. Any tendency on the part of a skater to try to predominate over his partner and companions immediately destroyed the illusion of the four. The variety of movement made possible by the number of performers lent itself to unlimited and charming combinations.

155

Every year a crack four would make an effort to change its programme and this was one reason why this type of skating was so popular in competitions in North America around 1925. It was the branch that was making the most progress. The Connaught Cup competition first presented in 1912 by the Duke of Connaught while Governor General of Canada was a stimulus to four-skating. One of the main reasons also was diversity. In competition there was a certain monotonous resemblance in the programmes of individual skating and even in the pairs, whereas fours presented greater variety. In addition it was necessary to be far more exact when skating in a group and this undoubtedly helped North American skating at a time when the art had only just been taken seriously in hand by the newly founded United States Figure Skating Association.

Fours continued to flourish in Canada and contribute to precision-inspired skating that in present times has been a feature of that country.

Shadow-skating and Lifts

Pair-skating which had been officially recognized by the International Skating Union in 1908 when the first World Championship in that event was staged in St Petersburg, continued to be practised for the next fifteen years along the classic lines of its inception. Three schools of influence combined in designing the classic expression of pair-skating at the beginning of the century.

The English school which very early furnished world champions in this branch emphasized a pleasing choreographic structure of programme executed with a certain technical precision. The Viennese school which introduced spirals and spins into pair programmes concentrated on dance steps speedily and gracefully executed. The German school whose representatives captured the first world pair title gave full expression to the movement of limbs producing a theatrical effect.

The English champions, Mr and Mrs Johnson, concentrated on moulding these three ideas and so set the pattern of international pair-skating. Elegance and ease was a feature of these early pair demonstrations which concentrated on varieties of spirals, centre figures which were classic school figure combinations that later grew into field figures, dance steps and to close the programme a spin and a jump or two. These latter combinations were not necessary to a pair programme. Athletics had not yet found their true place in pair-skating, for the risk of spoiling a neat and gracefully executed exhibition by a jump not in unison was too great to speculate upon. Considerable importance was put on the choreographic side, and a theatrical approach in presenting the programme was stressed.

After the First World War stagy and ornamental effects were dropped and pair-skating took on a formal expression that lacked personality.

Women now skated on a par with men and it was no longer necessary for the strong male to temper his virility and pace to allow his partner to complete the figure with him.

'Field figures', inspired from the original English combined-skating, were developed to cover wide stretches of the rink with each partner performing the same figures in unison but far apart. Some time earlier two English brothers demonstrated an idea of individual skating side by side executing the same figures very closely. They linked up various turns with quick moving steps and a simple jump or two with great precision and elegance. When the English pair, T. D. Richardson and his wife, executed almost an entire programme on these lines in 1923 a controversy started among the leading skaters as to whether to condemn or approve it as an interpretation of pair-skating. A noted journalist called it 'shadow-skating' and this title has stuck and expresses exactly what it is. Some authorities would not even look at it, believing it not to be pair-skating at all, others thought it the highest form of pair-skating. It was more difficult to perform, and when the future World Champions, Pierre Brunet and Andrée Joly of France, developed it to a high standard and incorporated it in their programme, shadow-skating became a classic department of pair-skating art.

Another additional movement of importance to pair-skating

was established at the same time, namely lifts. The first World Champions, the giant German Heinrich Burger had practised lifting his minute partner Anna Hübler in the air with considerable ease, and other leading skaters followed suit. It was regarded then as a strong man's feat and it was generally only tall men with tiny partners, or skaters with weight-lifting qualities that put it into practice.

Pierre Brunet was a tall man, six feet in height, and his partner *petite* and in 1924 they startled the skating world by their daring lifts. Then Otto Kaiser of Austria, who was an amateur weight-lifter, made an even deeper impression by lifting his partner Lily Scholz into the air with extraordinary ease.

As with shadow-skating, lifts were received with mixed feelings and regarded with distaste by many. Some looked upon lifts as acrobatics which did not belong to pure skating. There certainly was a crudity about them when first introduced, but no medium could be more adapted for expressing aerial grace than skating.

With the introduction of lifts and shadow-skating, to be coupled with the early ideas of skating hand-in-hand, pair-skating only now began to exist in a complete form. From now on it had a classic basis upon which to develop. It promised to be the most complete form in skating art.

PART FOUR

MODERN TIMES

CHAPTER 19

The First Skating Heroine

UNTIL 1924 the practice of artistic skating had been a rather timid affair. It was enjoyed wherever there were skating rinks by an elegant *élite* of adults who concentrated particularly on the cutting of intriguing figures. It was a comparatively limited circle of enthusiasts and the national and international competitions that took place annually drew only small crowds of followers, and a smaller public, more curious than enthusiastic.

At a time when other sports were being revolutionized by the dynamic qualities belonging to the twentieth century proper, artistic skating remained a pleasant winter pastime with appeal principally for those who indulged in it.

No sport however can hope to reach the real public today without a hero or heroine whose unparalleled exploits have captivated their imagination.

During the 1924 winter Olympic Games at Chamonix, the appearance of a child of eleven years old in the ladies' competition created a sensation. This plumpish fair-haired little girl attired in a dress that did not reach the knee, was making her *début* in international competition. Her unlimited confidence in herself seemed inspired by an extraordinary belief in the movements she was doing. What at first suggested a childlike arrogance was a new interpretation of skating, in artistry as well as in idea. Skating was to have Sonja Henie, which meant it was to have a future.

She was not only on the brink of personal success, and about to remodel women's skating, but more important, she was to make the art of artistic skating known and appreciated throughout the world. During the decade when she dominated women's skating, she was talked about in parts of the world which had never witnessed skating.

She won her first international title on a highly disputed decision, and her last in the same manner, but during a decade she took eight European titles, three Olympic Gold Medals and was Champion of the World for ten years running. During this decade she was unbeatable in competition, and brilliant in hundreds of exhibitions. This fair-haired Norwegian with the sparkling smile and engaging personality, converted thousands to practise skating as a pastime and inspired a new generation of skaters to imitate her.

After her Olympic victory in 1936 she left the world of amateur competition, to turn professional.

Through her outstanding exploits she brought ice-skating on to the sports pages of the daily press, and as a great champion of a sport she dominated so long and so brilliantly she made the art of ice-skating known on the front pages of the world's leading reviews.

She was dubbed 'Queen of the Ice', an outstanding figure in the world of sport. Ice-skating now had a heroine—a name and symbol giving universal inspiration.

The Contribution of Sonja Henie

When Sonja Henie took part in her first international competition, the winter Olympic Games at Chamonix in 1924, she was eleven years old. She was a sensation because a child had never competed before against mature adults. She was also sensational in everything about her, by what she wore, and what she did and how she did it.

She had been entered in this important international competition as the Norwegian champion to get experience. She finished last but one judge placed her first in the free skating. That was another sensation. She skated with a childlike swagger that gave a sort of unusual power to her gyrations and throughout her programme she adopted an athletic tone rather than a soft poetic manner that artistic skating was used to till then. The

162

judge who placed her first on his card foretold the future of skating. For its full development it needed much younger artists whose physical condition would be able to accomplish with the necessary ease all the athletic movements that could become possible in this art.

Artistic skating till now had been dominated by the important classic movements known as the school figures. Rightly so; free programmes based their whole interpretation upon elegance, precision and style, which the school figures emphasized. This resulted in a lyrical interpretation but an athletic manner was lacking. The finest exponents of that period, some of them indeed artists on ice, did employ athletic movements such as spins and jumps, and Gillis Grafström brought the Axel Paulsen jump to a standard of perfection, but these were all lacking in vigour.

Ice-skating development was limited now by age. Although there were, and always will be exceptions in a sport where a veteran surpasses youth in talent and execution, the prime age of a skater at that period was too high.

Skating was in need now of vigour, a 'punch' to be introduced into it, to move it on from its purely lyrical stage. It had been developed to its present point by mature adults who had worked out over a century the essential movements—they had found and established 'poetry of movement'.

Sonja Henie showed the way. She exhibited the enormous potentialities of youth, for when she won the World Championship in 1927 in her home town in Oslo at the age of thirteen over her adult rivals, youth was permanently established in the development of skating.

The general public were eager to see her, and the skating world now resigned itself to intelligent acceptance of a talented child among their ranks, and awaited with interest her next important appearance in competition. It was in the winter Olympic Games of 1928 at St Moritz where Sonja Henie gave the 'new look' to skating.

Like Jackson Haines, she had studied ballet, and herself mentioned that she had been 'saturated' in it. Like Haines it

163

was her first love, but unlike him she did not let it dominate her entire skating. She was too young then to reproduce the matured movements of ballet in her athletic ideas on the ice. She used all the advantages of youth to this purpose, she aimed too to blend this highly athletic element with pure artistic skating, as introduced by Haines. She introduced pattern into her free programmes. Until now the highest interpretation of individual skating was expressed by little more than variations of school figures linked up with simple stunt movements. Sonja Henie sought 'to tell a story'. She planned her programme on a dance choreography and gave form to the whole. Jumps and spins were no longer stunt movements isolated between Rockers or Counters. She gave flow to the sequences of different figures and meaning to the programme. Apart from remodelling women's skating, she 'refashioned' it as well. The athletic element she introduced into skating could not be performed with ankle-length skirts and wide hats. Sonja Henie brought in the short skirt which enabled girl skaters to indulge in any movement unhampered.

The Decade of Sonja Henie
Crowds gathered to see this 'child wonder' on ice, and international competition began to be an important event and as she won world title after world title through her technique and brilliance as a skater, she won over by her charm and strong personality a wider public following each year. Her name not only dominated women's skating but world skating. Yet she was not alone in competition. Fine skaters rich in talent from the United States, Canada, Austria and Sweden crowded on her heels, but she reigned supreme.

When she gave exhibitions, there was always a young enthusiast who would want to be like her, and a very young English girl named Cecilia Colledge was just one of them. She was to be the second youngster to cause a real sensation in the skating world. It took place at Garmisch-Partenkirchen during the Olympic Games in 1936. Sonja had been on top for ten years and now a fifteen-year-old challenged her supremacy. Sonja had

164

become almost a legend in the eyes of the general public and the first mention of the possibility of her being dethroned brought 200,000 people around the rink to ensure that it was not true. However, Sonja came out the Olympic Champion for the third time.

But, the little girl who had wanted to be like her, now threatened to eclipse her. The actual championship had been skated out in a tense atmosphere of competition. The result has been a subject of controversy in skating circles ever since. What really was important was that this youthful challenger brought into the sport a new type of skating. Inspired by the brilliant Sonja, Cecilia added to her grace a cold exactness in her movements and stunts that produced a sort of skating machine.

Throughout the decade in which Sonja Henie reigned supreme, the art of ice-skating was developing along a sound basis of classicism. It now had a definite form to follow. The period became rich in talent and artistic skating began to be spirited and precise.

The United States and Canada now sent over regularly their best representatives and in Maribel Vinson, Cecil Eustace Smith and Constance Wilson, the lively and vigorous characteristics of the New World began to shape and create the future American school. Austria with Fritzi Burger, Melitta Brunner, Karl Schäfer and others, strengthened the Vienna school which as a body was already the most powerful influence in skating. Vivi-Anne Hultén made bold attempts to carry the name of Sweden again to the heights that Grenander and Salchow had previously done. Then came the English challenge, very young and disciplined and technically nearer perfection than any of the others.

The outstanding feature of this decade was the increase in athletic ability on the part of the women. They were now able through the change in style of their clothes to show their skill and courage and skate on equal terms with the men. No longer need they be overshadowed by the male, but in contrast they could compete with him. This produced a revolution in the branch of pair-skating.

165

In 1936 the German pair, Maxi Herber and Ernst Baier, who won the Olympic event that year illustrated how complete a woman skater's repertoire was. Using shadow-skating, the most difficult branch of pair-skating, and employing it as their principal mode of expression, combining steps and jumps and spins, performing them in perfect unison, they showed a real advance in skating art. They were both individual performers of world-standard class and as a pair they will always rank as one of the great combinations in the sport. Apart from their artistry, they emphasized the need to incorporate individual skating in a pair demonstration to make it a satisfactory whole.

CHAPTER 20

The Rise of the English School

WHEN Sonja Henie retired from the amateur world of ice-skating she left behind a tradition that was to be followed by all the leading skaters of the future. Artistic skating was now a serious business for those who aspired to the highest honours. Planned training and plenty of it was the only way to achieve a good result. Sonja Henie may claim to be the first to have originated a clear-cut workmanlike method, and the first to emphasize its importance.

The opening of a number of modern covered rinks in London and elsewhere in England gave the opportunity to English skaters to train regularly. A nucleus of knowledgeable and experienced skating teachers made it possible to work seriously all the year round, and the English did so. They followed the example of Sonja Henie and started young, some even younger than she was.

Bernard Adams, who had been a fine English skating stylist and who turned to the practice and teaching of the international style shortly after its introduction into England, cannot be claimed as the founder of the modern English school, but he must be considered as a guide in the important transitionary period between the English and international styles. He taught with intelligence, and through the introduction of his own theories modern English skating took on a special character.

A German-Swiss, named Jacques Gerschwiler, came to England during the Henie days, as a private coach to the young Cecilia Colledge. He believed in pure technique almost to the exclusion of artistry. He became the founder of the English school, the modern scientific school of skating. Cold and almost dulless technique made its appearance in the big international

167

competitions significantly when competitor after competitor began to dominate the solo-skating world.

This approach produced a machine-like skater—both powerful and reliable. But individual personal expression became practically non-existent. This was clearly apparent among the men, who had not the natural charm of the female skater to soften a highly skilful performance and yet there was a peculiar fascination about this frigid manner of skating, but it had to be well-nigh perfect to give the desired effect. Cecilia Colledge as a technician was near this point and her interpretation possessed a cold charm through its power and meticulousness. She was the ideal type of competition skater, and the English school built its strength around this pattern. They worked upon the theme that full expression in this very difficult art could only be achieved by perfect technique, and this could only be acquired by the exclusion of nearly everything else.

All unnecessary effort was slowly eliminated, like the brutal pulled 'S' change of edge, and a general tidying up in the neat closing of the circles was effected.

Cecilia Colledge won the World Championship in 1937 and Megan Taylor,[4] another product of the disciplined English school came second. They were both the same age, and they were the first skaters in the world who made the World Championships into an event of colourful international sporting appeal. Megan won the following year and both in England and abroad these two brilliant rivals were to tussle for the highest honours and caused heated discussion among the ever increasing skating public.

Each year the English school came more prominently into the amateur arena with further fine examples of technical skating skill and the following year Daphne Walker took the third place of honour in the World Championships with Megan Taylor again the title-holder. Graham Sharp, the male counterpart, the purest of the English technical school, was Champion of the

[4] Megan Taylor was trained in equally as severe a way as Cecilia Colledge was, by her father Phil Taylor, the show-skater of repute.

World, and another Englishman, Freddie Tomlins, was second.

Then came the Second World War to halt competition and to slow down skating development in Europe.

But in wartime London ice-rinks carried on, and the English school gathered impetus. It was fortunate to be endowed with fine teachers; among others, Jacques Gerschwiler's brother Arnold, who had come to England previous to the outbreak of the war, emphasized his brother's principles. The founder's most outstanding pupil, Gladys Hogg, became the first woman teacher in the world to equal the highest pedagogic qualities of the male, and together this powerful trio turned out an *élite* of pupils.

By intense study and aim at technical perfection the English school laid a solid foundation upon which a wider development of the art could confidently take place.

Dancing on Ice

This had been a general term in skating circles in the early days as the designation of pair-skating and until about 1924 this latter form of skating expression was in fact dancing. Dancing on ice was also used with reference to Sonja Henie's free-skating performances, for the delicately graceful movements of the champion. But ballroom dancing upon the ice to special dance tunes had not yet been really developed.

It will be remembered how the Viennese tried to transplant it directly on to the ice without taking into consideration technical difficulties of this different art. But from that date the idea of dancing in ballroom fashion on ice has fascinated every artistic skating enthusiast. At the same time around 1890 when the skating waltz had been discovered, the Schöller march or ten-step made its appearance and both these excellent dances have been practised all over the skating world ever since.

Dancing in ballroom fashion, particularly waltzing, was considered one of the greatest delights in skating. It was considered easy, just a three to learn, and so anybody could do it.

After the success of the ten-step, another truly 'skating dance' made its appearance in Austria around 1909. It was called the

169

Kilian and needed a certain skill on skates to perform it at all. In the early twenties of this century in the United States and Canada where fours were popular and combined-skating had been practised, such group dances as the lancers and quadrilles were tried out. In England skaters endeavoured to combine the waltz with the ten-step and dance to foxtrot music. But all these dances were still performed in the spirit of recreation, and even competitions in waltzing lacked a certain seriousness, for everybody joined in!

Three factors were to play a deciding role in developing this branch of ice-skating seriously—the covered rink, the orchestra and the evening skater. 'Dance intervals' took place during the skating sessions, when the waltz and ten-step were the only dances in the schedule. Then an early form of tango made a timid entrance.

It was in England in an atmosphere where ballroom dancing had a great vogue with dancing clubs everywhere, that dancing on ice had its beginnings and it was to become the centre of its development.

In 1930 it was so popular that a big London newspaper ran a series of strip photographs illustrating 'dancing on ice' with the headline, 'Waltzing is the ambition of every skater'. The evening enthusiast practically abandoned all other ideas of skating in order to achieve competency in rhythmical dancing.

There were only three dances, the waltz, ten-step and a side-by-side fourteen-step which was the Kilian, and looked upon as an exhibition dance.

At the Imperial Ice Rink at Purley, outside London, a dance evening was held in December 1931. It was in the nature of an ice ball, for each dancer received a *carnet de bal*. The dances were the waltz, ten-step, tango, all repeated in various order, and there were also three competitions for these dances. The evening terminated with a 'Paul Jones'.

Sometime later a fancy-dress ball took place at the Ice Club, Westminster, where a gay crowd danced on ice till two o'clock in the morning.

170

But the repertoire was always the same, tango, waltz, ten-step and a Paul Jones. So in April 1933, the National Skating Association organized a competition at the Ice Club, Westminster, for the discovery of new dances suitable for use in rink dance intervals, and for the first time in skating history the competition was open to both amateurs and professionals. From the many dances presented only the foxtrot survived. It was a creation of the professional skaters Eric van der Weyden and Eva Keats. Two months later a foxtrot competition for professionals was held at Queen's Ice Club. As many as seven types, or rather ideas, were presented and Eric Van der Weyden, partnered by E. Heathcote, won. It was afterwards introduced to the regular dance intervals as the Slow Fox skated to foxtrot music. The steps were considered easy, but required an hour or two's practice before it could be danced together. Dancing on ice was still not intended to be, or to grow into, an equally important and skilful art as the other branches of skating; but the invention of the foxtrot by two skaters of skill and experience, who were able to create a modern rhythmic dance incorporating the ballroom idea with true ice-skating technique, was an important contribution.

Another competition was promoted at the Ice Club to find out what new dances skaters might have tried out and which might prove popular. No fewer than twenty dances were presented and two of them were accepted. This competition emphasized again that dances upon ice had to be 'skated', for previously a great number of them had the appearance of being 'walked'. Dancing on ice meant more of the basic idea of sliding over the ice than any other branch in skating art. It was perhaps this fact that brought about such a large number of entries wishing to compete in the discovery of new dances at Streatham Ice Rink at the end of 1934, in a competition for amateur and professional pairs. If the amateur champions were superior in skill, the professionals were more experienced in ice matters. The only amateur inventor taking part in this competition was R. J. Wilkie, who was to share with Van der Wcyden and Eva Keats

171

almost the entire honour of inventing modern ice-dancing.

As these competitions became more numerous and more popular a schedule of modern ice-dances came into being. A wave of enthusiasm swept over all the ice-rinks in England and dancing on ice became one of the most popular pastimes in the country. By 1939 thirteen dances were skated in the regular intervals, National Skating Association tests had been initiated and the first Amateur Championships of England were held in 1937. Ice-dancing had come to stay.

Ballet on Ice

Ever since Jackson Haines demonstrated the beauty of movement when gliding over ice in employing graceful ballet attitudes, many ambitious and skilful skaters have dreamt of interpreting true 'ballet' on ice.

In 1937 a daring artistic as well as commercial venture was introduced in London when the Royal Opera House at Covent Garden staged the world's first ice-ballet. It was mainly through the enthusiasm of Alfred Megroz, a prominent Swiss skater and former champion who had taught both ballet and skating that *Enchanted Night* and *The Brahmin's Daughter* saw the light of day. He sought to combine the principles of ballet and skating, a unification as he believed of art and sport. He made the vital mistake of not understanding that skating was not only a sport but an art as well, a very different art from ballet.

A £10,000 ice plant, the biggest ever built for a stage rink at that time, was installed at Covent Garden. A symphony orchestra of fifty and a cast of 120 skaters were engaged. Outstanding skaters for the star roles were employed: Andrée Joly and Pierre Brunet, one-time World Champions and Olympic winners, Phil Taylor, the man who could leap over a set of nine barrels, the young Belita who had represented England in the Olympic Games at the age of thirteen and turned professional at fourteen specially to star in this ballet, and Freda Whittaker who publicity claimed had 'skated in every capital of the world'. Technically everything was set for a 'grand slam'. The Queen of

Spain was in the Royal box. Tiaras glittered in the stalls and smoking was allowed, a rare thing at Covent Garden. Socially this first night was as good as opera itself. But artistically it was a flop and financially a disaster. As this chapter is only interested in the aesthetic side of the production let us see the reasons why this first 'ballet on ice' was a sad failure.

Alfred Megroz's idea was to wed what he called the two most graceful arts. As a skater he had been more of a musical interpreter on ice and not an athletic performer.

The actors in those ballets, *Enchanted Night* conceived by Alfred Megroz and *The Brahmin's Daughter*, an oriental fantasy based on the opera *Lakme*, were skaters, and the stars represented the art in its latest trend—the athletic. These performers needed space, they were cramped on a stage fifty-five by seventy feet, and obliged to execute too many movements 'on the spot'. The essential of skating art, 'gliding or sliding' was lost. The *corps de ballet*, too numerous for such a stage, crowded and collided, showing to a disastrous degree the failure on the part of the director to grasp the artistic aim of skating.

The ambitious organizers made the mistake of trying to imitate the existing customs of ballet, instead of constructing an art form out of the natural possibilities of skating.

So much for the skating side. It is now interesting to quote the opinion of an eminent ballet critic, Arnold L. Haskell, who attended that memorable night at Covent Garden when the fine art of skating forgot for a moment its place in the world of arts and insolently tried to imitate an older and more perfect sister.

Arnold L. Haskell wrote[5]:

> 'These skating "ballets" showed all the faults that the ballet proper has rid itself of these last twenty-five years.
>
> 'The first drama was a romantic story, blend of *Lac des Cygnes*, *Hansel and Gretel* and all the rest. The convention was for the performers to be on skates. Up to a certain

---

[5] (From the Appendix of the first edition of *BALLET PANORAMA* by Arnold L. Haskell published by B. T. Batsford Ltd, 1938)

173

point well and good. Fokine postulates *an equal partnership between the arts composing ballet*. One of the main criticisms of the skaters was made on that very point. The music was so subservient that the *tempo* was allowed to be tortured to an altogether unbearable degree. It no longer had an existence of its own.

'Noverre postulates *a relationship between movement and the action of the story*. In this romantic ballet a skater who excels at the feat and purely because he excels at the feat jumps over several obstacles clumsily deposited by the *corps de ballet*. This is the very *divertissement* entrance in the ballet that Noverre fought against. It was an excellent "stunt" in itself and could have been used dramatically, but the drama it provided was something quite extraneous to the story and that depended on the fear that the skater would hurt himself and the relief when he came to a halt in safety.

'The second ballet offended in more and in other respects. The scene was laid in India. Now the convention we have accepted up to a point is that the performers move on skates, but we have only accepted this up to a point. Both Noverre and Fokine *invoke a type of naturalism and insist that the action shall be plausible*. Ice under the burning tropical sun may be acceptable to some, but what is not is an Indian crowd in solid boots. Whatever the action that must appear ridiculous and the choice of scene was so extreme that there could be no two opinions. It was clearly a case of skating for the sake of skating—and excellent much of it was.

'*Movement also must fit the style of the work*. It is quite impossible even to approximate oriental movement on skates'.

Sonja Henie Again

When Sonja Henie retired from amateur competition she did not intend to retire from skating. She loved it too much. She had confidence in her ability and a blind faith in skating art.

She journeyed to the United States and plans were made for her to star in a skating act starting in New York and to tour nine cities going as far west as Minneapolis.

On her arrival in New York, the newspapers welcomed her as 'Norway's Pavlova of the ice'. The New York public, however, did not show a particular interest in the idea of the World and Olympic Ice Champion giving a show on ice. There had already been big demonstrations of champion American amateur skaters in the city and these gyrations on ice, though admired, did not set the town on fire. But Sonja Henie had it in her head to become a 'show-girl' on ice, a star in Hollywood. The first night of the show a crowd filtered into Madison Square Garden, prepared to yawn at another ice-skating show. But Sonja Henie was not only a champion skater, she had irresistible appeal. As she had transformed amateur skating overnight and made it into a sport of world appeal, so on that opening night she made artistic skating into a spectacle of considerable theatrical attraction. She did not do much more than what the public had become used to in exhibition-skating, but her charm and grace, and the colour she gave to her performance made her a sensation. She was now a show-girl on Broadway.

During her tour she skated to packed houses and when completed she went to the 'Movie Capital' and rented the only ice-rink in Hollywood to put on her own show.

Artistic skating was little appreciated in this city of celluloid and was never considered for a moment by the movie giants as an interesting subject for the cinema. But Hollywood went to the show. The stars were there and so were the magnates. It had the atmosphere of a record-breaking Hollywood *première*. Inside four-foot high glittering letters spelled out the name of the evening's star performer, and the audience waited in expectancy. Then under the light of a single spotlight the little girl in white appeared. Four minutes later she was a Hollywood star overnight. It was hard for her to get off the ice, they wanted her back, and back again.

Hollywood at once became ice-minded and a few months later Sonja Henie was the star of the first great movie skating story, *One in a Million*, making the art of skating known and seen in every corner of the world.

Her financial success caused other champions to turn professional to star in ice-shows and try the movies. She had prolonged the artistic life of an ice-skater and enriched the art of skating.

37. BALLROOM SCENE IN *Cinderella on Ice.* A grandiose theatrical production in London's Empress Hall, which starred a number of famous ex-amateurs

38. (left) JACQUELINE DU BIEF. The French World Champion of 1952

39. (right) JUNE MARK-HAM AND COURTNEY JONES. These British champions romped away with the 1958 World Dance Championships

40. CAROL HEISS, AMERICAN LADIES' CHAMPION. At thirteen years of age she ranked fourth in the world. Today she is nineteen and holds four world titles

41. ALBA ROVIDA. Inspiration of this history, and inspiration to a host of skaters in Switzerland and her native Italy

CHAPTER 21

The End of an Era

THE Second World War interrupted international competition in Europe and halted its development there, but it did not stop skating. In war-torn Europe the ice-rinks remained open and a new generation of youngsters rose during the period of hostilities and when the first European Championships were staged in Davos in 1947 a strong representation in all three categories competed.

These championships were coloured by Barbara Ann Scott, a little Canadian girl from Ottawa who came, saw and conquered not only the lovers of skating, but the world. This trim five-foot-three blue-eyed blonde with a rosebud mouth became a cover-girl overnight. The public took her to their hearts—this new queen of the ice was again setting tongues wagging in admiration of the art.

Like a little doll to be looked at and not to be touched, she drew a delicate charm around all she did upon the ice and elsewhere. She was the most complete skater up till now. She produced her skilful and artistic expression of skating art as if from out of a box in which everything was perfectly packed and orderly. She portrayed the almost perfect picture of the accepted idea of pre-war skating aims with just one difference. Her polish in execution gave it a new lustre, a modern finish.

She outdistanced all her rivals and set a unique example in skating art by performing all she did flawlessly. Yet she was not a machine, nor an ordinary performer. She was an ideal skater, not so much a model to copy, as an ideal to dream about.

Although she gave an idea of what to expect in skating in the future by her outstanding spinning and a neat double Salchow jump, she definitely marked the end of a chapter and not the

177

beginning of one. She gave a very beautiful finished picture of skating development since Sonja Henie started to remodel it.

The same championship featured among the men, a man who was, if not in glamour, certainly in dignity and as an outstanding performer, her counterpart. He was Hans Gerschwiler, the finest member of the English school. A Swiss by nationality he had donned the skates as late as thirteen years old in Switzerland where his uncle Arnold Gerschwiler was coach, and so began an association which was never to be impaired. He followed his uncle to London, and under his guidance made a spectacular ascent in the skating world, passing the coveted and difficult National Skating Association Gold Medal test after twenty-one months' work on the ice.

At his first attempt in the Swiss Championships in 1938 he won and was some hundred points ahead of his nearest rival on figures alone. He remained in England during the whole of the Second World War, and when he competed in these first post-war European Championships he showed the finest example yet of the precision-like English school of figure-skating.

Hans Gerschwiler was a scientific skater. Every movement or move, either in figure or free was calculated technically. Its cold correctness had a powerful charm about it, because it was performed to well-nigh perfection. The aim of the English school had been achieved by Hans Gerschwiler. It was the most advanced expression till now of masculine skating skill. Apart from brilliant performance achieved through fine skill, a feature of this school was the covering of the entire ice by skating. Until now simple runs in preparation for getting a position or as momentum for a jump were often strewn all over the rink in wasteful fashion which dislocated the continuity of the exhibitions. Hans Gerschwiler pioneered the employment of intricate steps in relation to the other movements as an essential part of the programme.

There were other skaters of quality of the English school who crowded these championships but all were dulled by Barbara Ann Scott's faultless exhibitions. Solidly set upon a fine technique, poised and fairylike, she gave to skating art a delightful charm.

Richard Button

In the 1947 European Championships the glamorous American woman champion, Gretchen Van Zandt Merill, through her showy exhibitions gave some inkling of a new refreshing breath that was shortly to burst upon the skating world with the new American school.

The goal in international competition was primarily dominated by aiming to be a great figure-skater. Concentration on this point almost to an exaggerated degree stilted the free-skating element, yet Sonja Henie long ago had shown where the skating future really lay.

Over in the New World the Americans took a daring decision in putting the accent on free skating. This branch had not yet incorporated vigorous athleticism into its repertoire.

Freddie Tomlins of England, runner-up in the 1939 World Championships began a brilliant skating career as a speed champion. He became the first artistic skater to use speed on ice, courageously and unhesitatingly to get the most out of a jump. He was the first skater to successfully jump a double Salchow, one and three-quarter gyrations in the air—this was the beginning of a new era. During the Second World War he went to Canada when training with the Royal Air Force, and a number of exhibitions he gave for war charities set American skating minds to work. Inspired by this dynamic Englishman they introduced a real athletic element into the poetry of skating. It is true that the spectacular had been smouldering in American skating minds already in the late 1920s, but it did not break forth until an advanced idea of it had been perfected.

Again it was a Swiss, Gustave Lussi, who became the father of the American school. He had been a ski-jumper, he believed in height and length, and in Dick Button he had a pupil who could interpret these ideas to perfection.

Dick Button began seriously to skate at twelve years of age;

179

six years later he won the Olympic Gold Medal and became Skating Champion of the World. He made his first European appearance in Stockholm in the World Championships of 1947. Rumours travelled around skating circles of a young boy phenomenon from the United States. But none of these reports were taken seriously in Europe. Everyone expected a skater would every now and then bring in a new movement, no one expected a new idea in skating.

Dick Button introduced real athletics in the form of 'barrier' high jumps into skating. The strength and virility of his performance simply crashed into the sober circles of the ice world and staggered for a moment their conventional ideas. Dick Button was not an artist but an athlete on ice. From the very first step to the last of his championship programme he piled every ounce of muscle into a power display on skates.

Ever since the discovery of the Dutch roll more than three centuries back, ice-skating had developed upon the lines of artistic expression. Athletic moves in the form of jumps before Freddie Tomlins had attempted to make an athletic feat out of them were performed as part of an artistic whole. Dick Button continually used the ice for purely athletic purposes. The skaters before him used it for sliding, mainly as an artistic expression.

Dick Button did not shatter the art in skating but he staggered the skater with his revolutionary approach and especially by the power of his programme. He thrilled and set a new fashion. Through his application of the full use of the sliding surface of the ice he was able to perform a variety of gyrations in the air with speed and in flight impossible in any sport or art. He gave to skating its own *raison d'être*.

Double jumps, combinations of jumps and spins, speed and dash were to intrude into the art of skating in the wake of this great champion. For five years he returned to participate and conquer in the big international events and each year introduced new jumps, more complicated, more spectacular and more additions to skating art.

Dick Button showed the athletic possibilities of the sport. It was introduced by a brilliant technician who was not afraid of convention—it exploded upon the skating world already as a polished and finished article. It staggered for a moment but did not destroy. It was finally understood and accepted.

The Trend of Skating

The year 1948 was Olympic year. It was also the year of Barbara Ann Scott and Dick Button, National Champions of Canada and America, North American, European, World Champions and Olympic Gold Medallists. This record is unique.

The delicate little Canadian skater's polish and perfection in movement contrasted splendidly with the powerful feats of the dynamic American. Ice-skating had a great future. Both these skaters dominated all their rivals, yet behind them came much fine talent, which both in quantity and quality marks the beginning of a new chapter.

It was the last year in which leading artists presented their own individual interpretation of skating art. There was the American school, spectacular, showy and predominantly athletic, and the Canadian school, polished, charming and supple. The English were there in force with their cold and meticulous science, their strength lay in the classic school figures, giving power and beauty to this section. The Austrians and the Hungarians showed their love for the interpretation of music in skating. The Czechs, the avant garde of double jumps in Europe, thrilled with their speed. The newly formed French school under the guidance of Jacqueline Vaudecrane gave a lively, spontaneous and promising display—this Olympic stage was a real international gathering.

The influence of the new American school of athletics had not yet been absorbed, and when it was, it was not immediately understood. It became a craze everywhere in Europe to jump, and this idea dominated the older skating schools to an exaggerated degree, and a wave of forced athleticism invaded the more elegant forms of skating. Jumping appeared for a time to be in the minds of many the sole object in skating.

Dick Button contributed and inspired—he could not be imitated, his skating was too personal. He had made skating a highly athletic art, but he had not converted it into a sport. This was the factor that was not realized generally until Hayes Alan Jenkins of America, successor to Dick Button after he retired, showed the beauty and elegance of a glide blended with outstanding athletic feats, the whole performed immaculately to music, the entire programme an artistic triumph. Hayes Alan Jenkins was an artist on ice.

At the same time there came upon the scene a girl with personality and artistry: Jacqueline Du Bief, champion of France, who dazzled and shocked at the same time, for unlike Dick Button who came with his 'revolution' all perfectly packed, labelled and ready, the refreshing ideas of Jacqueline Du Bief were born and experimented with during her climb to the top of international competition.

It became a battle royal between her and Jeannette Altwegg, champion of England. This skater will go down in skating history as the finest school figure skater of post-war times. She had a natural facility, ease and skill, that lent real beauty to this branch of the art. Her competence did not end there. She was a free skater of considerable power. She was above all, orthodox. She echoed the classic conception of an ice-skater's complete armament in a high degree.

Jacqueline Du Bief was an inspired artist seeking an outlet in skating. She performed feats of skill not only with her limbs. Her intensive spirit dominated. She showed by her brilliance and natural talent as an artist the wide possibilities of artistic skating, but more than anything else she brought a much needed refreshing air to the framework of women's skating. She appeared at the right time.

For two seasons the French and English champions clashed in nearly every major international competition—the fire and inspiration of one contrasting with the classic sobriety of the other.

Skating was passing through a phase of hesitation, but Hayes Alan Jenkins answered all the doubtful questions. With a superior technique to the French World Champion and an artistic feeling of expression unknown by the English Olympic Gold Medallist, he blended science with sentiment, athletics with elegance and proved skating to be an art.

The athletic element in a more poetic way came into pair-skating at the same time, a result of Dick Button's influence being the aim to stay poised in the air as long as possible. Double lifts, some of them strangely beautiful in their floating grace, were introduced into this branch. The trend of skating had become predominantly athletic.

The Role of Music in Free Skating

Ever since Jackson Haines emphasized the importance of musical accompaniment, music has remained an accessory to the skater's repertoire. In Vienna military bands played often at the ice-rinks—an additional attraction to skaters and setting the fashion throughout Central Europe.

But music was in this case only a background to the skater's enjoyment gliding over the ice, and music remained a background, with few exceptions, until very recent times.

In 1911, the reigning lady Champion of the World, Lily Kronberger of Hungary, came to the World Championships in Vienna bringing with her from Budapest a military band, specially for accompanying her free-skating programme. This marks a very important point in the story of skating, for Lily Kronberger realized that a free-skating programme should interpret the music chosen, which was essential in such skating.

Lily Kronberger skated to the *Pas des Patineurs* and her interpretation of the music allied to skating skill was much admired.

It is a curious fact that after Lily Kronberger's experiment musical interpretation did not receive the important place it should have among the leading skaters that were to follow. For more than three decades music remained in the background of free-skating programmes, with only weak attempts at musical interpretation, generally the work of musically gifted performers, such as Karl Schäfer, the brilliant Viennese World Champion, who was an accomplished violinist.

183

It was in 1948 during the winter Olympic Games that another girl, Marylyn Take of Canada, took a very bold step at musical interpretation, presenting a programme largely dominated by ballet movements. Her performance was beautiful and it showed clearly that skating in its highest form must interpret music.

There followed a year or so of experiment. The post-war introduction of virile athleticism by the Americans sent the European skaters on a jumping 'spree' and in an attempt to blend this with musical interpretation, a complete misunderstanding of values ensued. Skaters liked music now with a 'boom' in it and tried to land a double jump to coincide with these 'booms'. This sensationalism became an obsession until the American male skaters at the World Championships in London in 1950 illustrated a unique combination of daring athletics, musically interpreted, throughout five minutes of high-powered skating.

It was the Americans and Canadians that now made attempts to adapt their performances to the music chosen. Each skater had his specially cut gramophone record, and this soon became commonplace among European skaters too.

CHAPTER 22

First Ice Dance Championships

RHYTHMIC dancing on ice in ballroom fashion was given official recognition by the International Skating Union in 1952 when the first World Championships in this special branch took place in Paris together with the other sections of artistic skating.

Ever since competitive skating returned after the termination of the Second World War, rhythmic dancing on ice had been discussed by skating leaders as requiring a place in international competitions. The governing authorities were hesitant. This was a form of skating the English practised and in which they were already specialists. Memories of the particular 'English style' clouded and haunted national and international opinion. Was it not another odd English idea? Further, with the introduction of revolutionary movements since Dick Button broke on to the scene, the ruling authorities had almost lost touch with the trend of skating development. Ideas were being born too fast and they were unable to grasp and control the new developments.

However, it did get a showing in the Wembley Stadium in London on the occasion of the World Championships in 1950. It was termed an international dance championship and the United States, followers of the English in this domain, sent three pairs to compete against the three English 'cracks'. The demonstrations were dull but there was a sensation in that the English were defeated. They were the more spectacular, the Americans quieter and very precise.

The competition was composed of four dances chosen from the repertoire of the scheduled classical dances and a free-dancing programme of the competitors' own invention. This

185

policy has not been changed. The exhibitions of the compulsory dances were all executed to uniform pattern. They were technically uninteresting with the exception of the intriguing American waltz, seen for the first time in a big competition in England, which by its unusualness caused heavy and rather unfair criticism by the English, But it is now included in the International Skating Union's schedule for World Championships.

The free dancing had not yet a real form. The Americans presented three minutes of somewhat dull stepping and turns very neatly executed. The English entered with a timid imitation of pair-skating performed rhythmically to music which included a number of combinations of dancing jumps, but the general reception was cold. The authorities might have left the idea of dance championships alone for a while, but the English, who first believed in this new branch, and secondly were practically the inventors and masters of modern ice-dancing, were smarting under this unexpected defeat. They had to have another opportunity of showing their qualities to the full and perhaps avenging this set-back. This enthusiasm brought about the second international competition in ice-dancing which, running concurrently with the World Championships in Milan, took place the following year. It was truly international, with Belgium, Holland, Switzerland and Austria competing. England sent a completely new team over, two young pairs with dash, style, technique and ideas. The Americans, as before, were neat and slow.

Against the Anglo-Saxon masters the Continentals appeared more courageous than scientific, but they brought colour to the competition by their gaiety, and some even brought ideas. Lawrence Demmy partnering Jean Westwood won the competition for England. John Slater and Joan Dewhurst took second place. Some way behind came the Americans and then the Continentals. But the English couples demonstrated a vast superiority in skill over their nearest rivals, but above all they showed what rhythmic dancing on ice could be. Their brilliant performances in Milan assured this new branch of skating its

186

rightful place. The World Championships were scheduled for the following year.

Europe and America now followed to the letter the English style of dancing, a strong accent being placed upon technique and a rigidity of style in the classic dances.

It was in free dancing that a sense of direction was lacking. Each year the leading English pair became more daring and in 1953 presented a free-dancing programme with complicated skating lifts and other coupled movements which resembled pair-skating more than dancing. Performed with splendid harmony to musical accompaniment it actually surpassed much of the best pair work. But the original idea of rhythmic dancing on ice was lost. It was being turned into an athletic demonstration pure and simple, an impertinent imitation of pair-skating. So new rules were brought in. Lifts were abolished, spins were shortened and dancing on ice was to return to its original conception of fifty years ago, hand-in-hand skating.

The English still occupied the first places in international competition. The Americans still neat but lacking in ideas stayed put, while the Continentals began to creep up close to them.

In 1954 the first European Championships in rhythmic ice-dancing took place in Bolzano, Italy, emphasizing the growing importance of the new branch. France, Italy and Germany now swelled the ranks in these competitions.

Rhythmic ice-dancing now settled down to pursuing the English idea of fine technique with a sacrifice of mood and feeling. This will have to be enriched by a more complete repertoire of movements before it can develop to the full and become an equal to the other branches in skating art.

Ice-skating Now

$100,000 for Ronald Robertson, a triple Axel jump by David Jenkins—this is skating now.

Theatrical ice-entertainment sweeping across two continents in winter and summer alike drawing hundreds of thousands of enthusiastic spectators, acrobatic jumping to rival the greatest in trapeze thrills—all this is skating now.

The World Ice Hockey Championships have become a sporting event of great public appeal. Artistic skating through four centuries of practice has developed into an art of universal appeal.

Through artificial ice-rinks, climate no longer matters and skating is practised in Japan and New Zealand, in Africa and Australia as well as in the cold lands of the North.

The *élite* in the art are personalities for the front pages of the world's press. The great names echo throughout the world as inspiration for further progress.

Jackson Haines swayed to the lilt of melody. Sonja Henie came to give the sport what it needed most, a popular heroine. Barbara Ann Scott passed by, fairylike yet real, a legend of modern times. After that, the great Dick Button, athletic and powerful, a fitting emblem for this atomic age. Then Tenley Albright, the feminine athlete who danced and thrilled. Gloria Nord, the 'show-girl', one hundred per cent 'skating glamour' and Carol Heiss, the speedy, lively, dashing champion who bagged a hat trick of maximum sixes in the World Championships, a record requiring perfect execution.

All this is skating now.

APPENDIX A

NAMES OF INVENTORS OF MODERN ICE-DANCING WITH DATES OF FIRST OFFICIAL PERFORMANCES

(Dances arranged in order of international classification)

1. FOURTEEN-STEP .. **Franz Schöller**
   (Ice-rink of the *Wiener Eislauf Vereins*, Vienna, 1889, called the Schöller March)

2. FOXTROT .. .. **Eric van der Weyden and Eva Keats**
   (Westminster Ice Rink, London, 1933)

3. ROCKER-FOXTROT .. **Eric van der Weyden and Eva Keats**
   (Streatham Ice Rink, London, 1934)

4. EUROPEAN WALTZ .. **Not established**
   (Before 1900 but the date has never really been settled)

5. AMERICAN WALTZ .. **Not established, inventor or place**

6. WESTMINSTER WALTZ **Eric van der Weyden and Eva Keats**
   (Westminster Ice Rink, London, 1938)

7. VIENNESE WALTZ .. **Eric van der Weyden and Eva Keats**
   (Streatham Ice Rink, London, 1934)

8. KILIAN .. .. **Karl Schreiter**
   (Engelmann Ice Rink, Vienna, 1909)

9. QUICKSTEP .. .. **Reginald J. Wilkie and Daphne B. Wallis**
(Westminster Ice Rink, London, 1938)

10. PASO DOBLE .. .. **Reginald J. Wilkie and Daphne B. Wallis**
(Westminster Ice Rink, London, 1938)

11. TANGO .. .. **Paul Kreckow and Trudy Harris**
(Hammersmith Ice Rink, London, 1932)

12. ARGENTINE TANGO .. **Reginald J. Wilkie and Daphne B. Wallis**
(Westminster Ice Rink, London, 1934)

13. BLUES .. .. **Robert Dench and Lesley Turner**
(Streatham Ice Rink, London, 1934)

14. RUMBA .. .. **Walter Gregory**
(This dance is not included in the International Schedule)

APPENDIX B

LIST OF EUROPEAN CHAMPIONSHIP WINNERS

(a) Men's Championships

1891 Hamburg
    1. O. Uhlig, Germany
    2. A. Schmitson, Germany
    3. Franz Zilly, Germany

1892 Vienna
    1. Edward Engelmann, Austria
    2. Tibor von Földvary, Hungary
    3. Georg Zachariades, Austria

1893 No competition

1894 Vienna
    1. Edward Engelmann, Austria
    2. Gustav Hügel, Austria
    3. Tibor von Földvary, Hungary

1895 Budapest
    1. Tibor von Földvary, Hungary
    2. Gustav Hügel, Austria
    3. Gilbert Fuchs, Germany

1896 No competition

1897 No competition

1898 Trondheim
    1. Ulrich Salchow, Sweden
    2. Johan Lefstad, Norway
    3. Oskar Holthe, Norway

1899 Davos
    1. Ulrich Salchow, Sweden
    2. Gustav Hügel, Austria
    3. Ernst Fellner, Austria

1900 Berlin
    1. Ulrich Salchow, Sweden
    2. Gustav Hügel, Austria
    3. Oskar Holthe, Norway
1901 Vienna
    1. Gustav Hügel, Austria
    2. Gilbert Fuchs, Germany
    3. Ulrich Salchow, Sweden
1902 No competition
1903 No competition
1904 Davos
    1. Ulrich Salchow, Sweden
    2. Max Bohatsch, Austria
    3. N. Panin, Russia
1905 Bonn
    1. Max Bohatsch, Austria
    2. Heinrich Burger, Germany
    3. Karl Zenger, Germany
1906 Davos
    1. Ulrich Salchow, Sweden
    2. Ernst Herz, Austria
    3. Per Thorén, Sweden
1907 Berlin
    1. Ulrich Salchow, Sweden
    2. Gilbert Fuchs, Germany
    3. Ernst Herz, Austria
1908 Warsaw
    1. Ernst Herz, Austria
    2. N. Panin, Russia
    3. S. Przedrzymirski, Austria
1909 Budapest
    1. Ulrich Salchow, Sweden
    2. Gilbert Fuchs, Germany
    3. Per Thorén, Sweden
1910 Berlin
    1. Ulrich Salchow, Sweden

2. Werner Rittberger, Germany
3. Per Thorén, Sweden

1911 St Petersburg (Leningrad)
1. Per Thorén, Sweden
2. Karl Ollow, Russia
3. Werner Rittberger, Germany

1912 Stockholm
1. Gösta Sandahl, Sweden
2. Ivan P. Malinin, Russia
3. Martin Stixrud, Norway

1913 Christiania (Oslo)
1. Ulrich Salchow, Sweden
2. Andor Szende, Hungary
3. Willy Böckl, Austria

1914 Vienna
1. Fritz Kachler, Austria
2. Andr. Krogh, Norway
3. Willy Böckl, Austria

1915-1921 No competition

1922 Davos
1. Willy Böckl, Austria
2. Fritz Kachler, Austria
3. Ernst Oppacher, Austria

1923 Christiania (Oslo)
1. Willy Böckl, Austria
2. Martin Stixrud, Norway
3. Gunnar Jakobsson, Finland

1924 Davos
1. Fritz Kachler, Austria
2. Ludwig Wrede, Austria
3. Werner Rittberger, Germany

1925 Triberg
1. Willy Böckl, Austria
2. Werner Rittberger, Germany
3. Otto Preiszecker, Austria

1926 Davos
 1. Willy Böckl, Austria
 2. Otto Preiszecker, Austria
 3. Georg Gautschi, Switzerland
1927 Vienna
 1. Willy Böckl, Austria
 2. Hugo Distler, Austria
 3. Karl Schäfer, Austria
1928 Troppau
 1. Willy Böckl, Austria
 2. Karl Schäfer, Austria
 3. Otto Preiszecker, Austria
1929 Davos
 1. Karl Schäfer, Austria
 2. Georg Gautschi, Switzerland
 3. Ludwig Wrede, Austria
1930 Berlin
 1. Karl Schäfer, Austria
 2. Otto Gold, Czechoslovakia
 3. Markus Nikkanen, Finland
1931 Vienna
 1. Karl Schäfer, Austria
 2. Ernst Baier, Germany
 3. Hugo Distler, Austria
1932 Paris
 1. Karl Schäfer, Austria
 2. Ernst Baier, Germany
 3. Erich Erdös, Austria
1933 London
 1. Karl Schäfer, Austria
 2. Ernst Baier, Germany
 3. Erich Erdös, Austria
1934 Innsbruck
 1. Karl Schäfer, Austria
 2. Dénes Pataky, Hungary
 3. Elemér Terták, Hungary

1935 St Moritz
1. Karl Schäfer, Austria
2. Felix Kaspar, Austria
3. Ernst Baier, Germany

1936 Berlin
1. Karl Schäfer, Austria
2. Graham Sharp, Gt Britain
3. Ernst Baier, Germany

1937 Prague
1. Felix Kaspar, Austria
2. Graham Sharp, Gt Britain
3. Elemér Terták, Hungary

1938 St Moritz
1. Felix Kaspar, Austria
2. Graham Sharp, Gt Britain
3. Herbert Alward, Austria

1939 Davos
1. Graham Sharp, Gt Britain
2. Freddie Tomlins, Gt Britain
3. Horst Faber, Germany

1940-1946 No competition

1947 Davos
1. Hans Gerschwiler, Switzerland
2. Vladislav Cáp, Czechoslovakia
3. Fernand Leemans, Belgium

1948 Prague
1. Richard Button, USA [6]
2. Hans Gerschwiler, Switzerland
3. Edi Rada, Austria

1949 Milan
1. Edi Rada, Austria
2. Ede Király, Hungary
3. Helmut Seibt, Austria

1950 Oslo
1. Ede Király, Hungary

[6] Till 1948 the European Championships were also open to non-Europeans.

    2. Helmut Seibt, Austria
    3. Carlo Fassi, Italy
1951 Zürich
    1. Helmut Seibt, Austria
    2. Horst Faber, Germany
    3. Carlo Fassi, Italy
1952 Vienna
    1. Helmut Seibt, Austria
    2. Carlo Fassi, Italy
    3. Michael Carrington, Gt Britain
1953 Dortmund
    1. Carlo Fassi, Italy
    2. Alain Giletti, France
    3. Freimut Stein, Germany
1954 Bolzano
    1. Carlo Fassi, Italy
    2. Alain Giletti, France
    3. Karol Divin, Czechoslovakia
1955 Budapest
    1. Alain Giletti, France
    2. Michael Booker, Gt Britain
    3. Karol Divin, Czechoslovakia
1956 Paris
    1. Alain Giletti, France
    2. Michael Booker, Gt Britain
    3. Karol Divin, Czechoslovakia
1957 Vienna
    1. Alain Giletti, France
    2. Karol Divin, Czechoslovakia
    3. Michael Booker, Gt Britain
1958 Bratislava
    1. Karol Divin, Czechoslovakia
    2. Alain Giletti, France
    3. Alain Calmat, France
1959 Davos
    1. Karol Divin, Czechoslovakia

2. Alain Giletti, France
3. Norbert Felsinger, Austria

(b) Women's Championships

1930 Vienna
1. Fritzi Burger, Austria
2. Ilse Hornung, Austria
3. Vivi-Anne Hultén, Sweden
1931 St Moritz
1. Sonja Henie, Norway
2. Fritzi Burger, Austria
3. Hilde Holovski, Austria
1932 Paris
1. Sonja Henie, Norway
2. Fritzi Burger, Austria
3. Vivi-Anne Hultén, Sweden
1933 London
1. Sonja Henie, Norway
2. Cecilia Colledge, Gt Britain
3. Fritzi Burger, Austria
1934 Prague
1. Sonja Henie, Norway
2. Liselotte Landbeck, Austria
3. Maribel Vinson, USA
1935 St Moritz
1. Sonja Henie, Norway
2. Liselotte Landbeck, Austria
3. Cecilia Colledge, Gt Britain
1936 Berlin
1. Sonja Henie, Norway
2. Cecilia Colledge, Gt Britain
3. Megan Taylor, Gt Britain
1937 Prague
1. Cecilia Colledge, Gt Britain
2. Megan Taylor, Gt Britain
3. Emmy Puzinger, Austria

197

1938 St Moritz
1. Cecilia Colledge, Gt Britain
2. Megan Taylor, Gt Britain
3. Emmy Puzinger, Austria

1939 London
1. Cecilia Colledge, Gt Britain
2. Megan Taylor, Gt Britain
3. Daphne Walker, Gt Britain

1940-1946 No competition

1947 Davos
1. Barbara Ann Scott, Canada
2. Gretchen Van Zandt Merrill, USA
3. Daphne Walker, Gt Britain

1948 Prague
1. Barbara Ann Scott, Canada
2. Eva Pawlik, Austria
3. Alena Vrzanova, Czechoslovakia

1949 Milan
1. Eva Pawlik, Austria
2. Alena Vrzanova, Czechoslovakia
3. Jeannette Altwegg, Gt Britain

1950 Oslo
1. Aja Vrzanova, Czechoslovakia
2. Jeannette Altwegg, Gt Britain
3. Jacqueline Du Bief, France

1951 Zürich
1. Jeannette Altwegg, Gt Britain
2. Jacqueline Du Bief, France
3. Barbara Wyatt, Gt Britain

1952 Vienna
1. Jeannette Altwegg, Gt Britain
2. Jacqueline Du Bief, France
3. Barbara Wyatt, Gt Britain

1953 Dortmund
1. Valda Osborn, Gt Britain
2. Gundi Busch, Germany

3. Erica Batchelor, Gt Britain

1954 Bolzano
1. Gundi Busch, Germany
2. Erica Batchelor, Gt Britain
3. Yvonne Sugden, Gt Britain

1955 Budapest
1. Hanna Eigel, Austria
2. Yvonne Sugden, Gt Britain
3. Erica Batchelor, Gt Britain

1956 Paris
1. Ingrid Wendl, Austria
2. Yvonne Sugden, Gt Britain
3. Erica Batchelor, Gt Britain

1957 Vienna
1. Hanna Eigel, Austria
2. Ingrid Wendl, Austria
3. Hanna Walter, Austria

1958 Bratislava
1. Ingrid Wendl, Austria
2. Hanna Walter, Austria
3. Joan Haanappel, Holland

1959 Davos
1. Hanna Walter, Austria
2. Sjoujke Dijkstra, Holland
3. Joan Haanappel, Holland

(c) Pairs Championships

1930 Vienna
1. Olga Organista/Szandor Szalay, Hungary
2. Emilie Rotter/Laszlo Szollas, Hungary
3. Gisela Hochhaltinger/Otto Preiszecker, Austria

1931 St Moritz
1. Olga Organista/Szandor Szalay, Hungary
2. Emilie Rotter/Laszlo Szoelas, Hungary
3. Lilly Gaillard/Willy Petter, Austria

1932 Paris
1. Andrée and Pierre Brunet-Joly, France
2. Lilly Gaillard/Willy Petter, Austria
3. Idi Papez/Karl Zwack, Austria
1933 London
1. Idi Papez/Karl Zwack, Austria
2. Lilly Scholz-Gaillard/Willy Petter, Austria
3. Mollie Phillips/R. Murdoch, Gt Britain
1934 Prague
1. Emilie Rotter/Laszlo Szollas, Hungary
2. Idi Papez/Karl Zwack, Austria
3. Zofjz Bilorowna/Tadeusz Kowalski, Poland
1935 St Moritz
1. Maxi Herber/Ernst Baier, Germany
2. Idi Papez/Karl Zwack, Austria
3. Lucy Gallo/Reszoe Dillinger, Hungary
1936 Berlin
1. Maxi Herber/Ernst Baier, Germany
2. Violet and Leslie Cliff, Gt Britain
3. Piroska and Attilia Szekrényessy, Hungary
1937 Prague
1. Maxi Herber/Ernst Baier, Germany
2. Ilse and Erik Pausin, Austria
3. Piroska and Attilia Szekrényessy, Hungary
1938 Troppau
1. Maxi Herber/Ernst Baier, Germany
2. Ilse and Erik Pausin, Austria
3. Inge Koch/Günther Noack, Germany
1939 Zakopane
1. Maxi Herber/Ernst Baier, Germany
2. Ilse and Erik Pausin, Austria
3. Inge Koch/Günther Noack, Germany
1940-1946 No competition
1947 Davos
1. Micheline Lannoy/Pierre Baugniet, Belgium
2. Winifred and Dennis Silverthorne, Gt Britain

3. Suzanne Diskeuve/Edmond Verbustel, Belgium
1948 Prague
1. Andrea Kékessy/Ede Király, Hungary
2. B. Knittlová/K. Vosátika, Czechoslovakia
3. Herta and Emil Ratzenhofer, Austria
1949 Milan
1. Andrea Kékessy/Ede Király, Hungary
2. Marianne and Laszlo Nagy, Hungary
3. Herta and Emil Ratzenhofer, Austria
1950 Oslo
1. Marianne and Laszlo Nagy, Hungary
2. Eliane Steinemann/André Calame, Switzerland
3. Jennifer and John Nicks, Gt Britain
1951 Zürich
1. Ria Baran/Paul Falk, Germany
2. Eliane Steinemann/André Calame, Switzerland
3. Jennifer and John Nicks, Gt Britain
1952 Vienna
1. Ria and Paul Falk, Germany
2. Jennifer and John Nicks, Gt Britain
3. Marianne and Laszlo Nagy, Hungary
1953 Dortmund
1. Jennifer and John Nicks, Gt Britain
2. Marianne and Laszlo Nagy, Hungary
3. Sissy Schwarz/Kurt Oppelt, Austria
1954 Bolzano
1. Sylvia and Michel Grandjean, Switzerland
2. Sissy Schwarz/Kurt Oppelt, Austria
3. Sona Balunova/M. Balun, Czechoslovakia
1955 Budapest
1. Marianne and Laszlo Nagy, Hungary
2. Vera Suchankóva/Zdenek Dolezal, Czechoslovakia
3. Marika Kilius/Franz Ningel, Germany
1956 Paris
1. Sissy Schwarz/Kurt Oppelt, Austria
2. Marianne and Laszlo Nagy, Hungary

    3. Marika Kilius/Franz Ningel, Germany
1957 Vienna
    1. Vera Suchanková/Zdenek Dolezal, Czechoslovakia
    2. Marianne and Laszlo Nagy, Hungary
    3. Marika Kilius/Franz Ningel, Germany
1958 Bratislava
    1. Vera Suchanková/Zdenek Dolezal, Czechoslovakia
    2. Nina and Stanislas Zhuk, USSR
    3. Anthony Holles/Joyce Coates, Gt Britain
1959 Davos
    1. Marika Kilius/Hans-Jürgen Bäumler, Western Germany
    2 Nina and Stanislas Zhuk, USSR
    3. Joyce P. Coates/Anthony F. Holles, Gt Britain

(d) Ice-dancing Championships

1954 Bolzano
    1. Jean Westwood/Lawrence Demmy, Gt Britain
    2. Nesta Davies/Paul Thomas, Gt Britain
    3. Barbara Radford/Raymond Lockwood, Gt Britain
1955 Budapest
    1. Jean Westwood/Lawrence Demmy, Gt Britain
    2. Pamela Weight/Paul Thomas, Gt Britain
    3. Barbara Radford/Raymond Lockwood, Gt Britain
1956 Paris
    1. Pamela Weight/Paul Thomas, Gt Britain
    2. June Markham/Courtney Jones, Gt Britain
    3. Barbara Thompson/Gerald Rigby, Gt Britain
1957 Vienna
    1. June Markham/Courtney Jones, Gt Britain
    2. Barbara Thompson/Gerald Rigby, Gt Britain
    3. Catherine Morris/Michael Robinson, Gt Britain
1958 Bratislava
    1. June Markham/Courtney Jones, Gt Britain
    2. Catherine Morris/Michael Robinson, Gt Britain

3. Barbara Thompson/Gerald Rigby, Gt Britain

1959 Davos

1. Doreen Denny/Courtney Jones, Gt Britain
2. Catherine Morris/Michael Robinson, Gt Britain
3. Christiane and Jean Paul Guhel, France

APPENDIX C

LIST OF WORLD CHAMPIONSHIP WINNERS

(a) Men's Championships

1896 St Petersburg (Leningrad)
1. Gilbert Fuchs, Germany
2. Gustav Hügel, Austria
3. George Sanders, Russia

1897 Stockholm
1. Gustav Hügel, Austria
2. Ulrich Salchow, Sweden
3. Johan Lefstad, Norway

1898 London
1. Henning Grenander, Sweden
2. Gustav Hügel, Austria
3. Gilbert Fuchs, Germany

1899 Davos
1. Gustav Hügel, Austria
2. Ulrich Salchow, Sweden
3. Edgar Syers, Gt Britain

1900 Davos
1. Gustav Hügel, Austria
2. Ulrich Salchow, Sweden
3. —

1901 Stockholm
1. Ulrich Salchow, Sweden
2. Gilbert Fuchs, Germany
3. —

1902 London
1. Ulrich Salchow, Sweden
2. Mrs Madge Syers-Cave, Gt Britain
3. Martin Gordan, Germany

1903 St Petersburg (Leningrad)
1. Ulrich Salchow, Sweden
2. N. Panin (Kolomenkin), Russia
3. Max Bohatsch, Austria
1904 Berlin
1. Ulrich Salchow, Sweden
2. Heinrich Burger, Germany
3. Martin Gordan, Germany
1905 Stockholm
1. Ulrich Salchow, Sweden
2. Max Bohatsch, Austria
3. Per Thorén, Sweden
1906 Munich
1. Gilbert Fuchs, Germany
2. Heinrich Burger, Germany
3. Bror Meyer, Sweden
1907 Vienna
1. Ulrich Salchow, Sweden
2. Max Bohatsch, Austria
3. Gilbert Fuchs, Germany
1908 Troppau
1. Ulrich Salchow, Sweden
2. Gilbert Fuchs, Germany
3. Heinrich Burger, Germany
1909 Stockholm
1. Ulrich Salchow, Sweden
2. Per Thorén, Sweden
3. Ernst Herz, Austria
1910 Davos
1. Ulrich Salchow, Sweden
2. Werner Rittberger, Germany
3. Andor Szende, Hungary
1911 Berlin
1. Ulrich Salchow, Sweden
2. Werner Rittberger, Germany
3. Fritz Kachler, Austria

1912 Manchester
1. Fritz Kachler, Austria
2. Werner Rittberger, Germany
3. Andor Szende, Hungary
1913 Vienna
1. Fritz Kachler, Austria
2. Willy Böckl, Austria
3. Andor Szende, Hungary
1914 Helsingfors
1. Gösta Sandahl, Sweden
2. Fritz Kachler, Austria
3. Willy Böckl, Austria
1915-1921 No competition
1922 Stockholm
1. Gillis Grafström, Sweden
2. Fritz Kachler, Austria
3. Willy Böckl, Austria
1923 Vienna
1. Fritz Kachler, Austria
2. Willy Böckl, Austria
3. Gösta Sandahl, Sweden
1924 Manchester
1. Gillis Grafström, Sweden
2. Willy Böckl, Austria
3. Ernst Oppacher, Austria
1925 Vienna
1. Willy Böckl, Austria
2. Fritz Kachler, Austria
3. Otto Preiszecker, Austria
1926 Berlin
1. Willy Böckl, Austria
2. Otto Preiszecker, Austria
3. John F. Page, Gt Britain
1927 Davos
1. Willy Böckl, Austria
2. Otto Preiszecker, Austria

3. Karl Schäfer, Austria
1928 Berlin
1. Willy Böckl, Austria
2. Karl Schäfer, Austria
3. Hugo Distler, Austria
1929 London
1. Gillis Grafström, Sweden
2. Karl Schäfer, Austria
3. Ludwig Wrede, Austria
1930 New York
1. Karl Schäfer, Austria
2. R. Felix Turner, USA
3. Georg Gautschi, Switzerland
1931 Berlin
1. Karl Schäfer, Austria
2. R. Felix Turner, USA
3. Ernst Baier, Germany
1932 Montreal
1. Karl Schäfer, Austria
2. Montague Wilson, Canada
3. Ernst Baier, Germany
1933 Zürich
1. Karl Schäfer, Austria
2. Ernst Baier, Germany
3. Markus Nikkanen, Finland
1934 Stockholm
1. Karl Schäfer, Austria
2. Ernst Baier, Germany
3. Erich Erdös, Austria
1935 Budapest
1. Karl Schäfer, Austria
2. Jack Dunn, Gt Britain
3. Dénes Pataky, Hungary
1936 Paris
1. Karl Schäfer, Austria
2. Graham Sharp, Gt Britain

3. Felix Kaspar, Austria

1937 Vienna

1. Felix Kaspar, Austria
2. Graham Sharp, Gt Britain
3. Elemér Terták, Hungary

1938 Berlin

1. Felix Kaspar, Austria
2. Graham Sharp, Gt Britain
3. Herbert Alward, Austria

1939 Budapest

1. Graham Sharp, Gt Britain
2. Freddie Tomlins, Gt Britain
3. Horst Faber, Germany

1940-1946 No competition

1947 Stockholm

1. Hans Gerschwiler, Switzerland
2. Richard T. Button, USA
3. Arthur J. Apfel, Gt Britain

1948 Davos

1. Richard T. Button, USA
2. Hans Gerschwiler, Switzerland
3. Ede Király, Hungary

1949 Paris

1. Richard T. Button, USA
2. Ede Király, Hungary
3. Edi Rada, Austria

1950 London

1. Richard T. Button, USA
2. Ede Király, Hungary
3. Hayes Alan Jenkins, USA

1951 Milan

1. Richard T. Button, USA
2. James D. Grogan, USA
3. Helmut Seibt, Austria

1952 Paris

1. Richard T. Button, USA

2. James D. Grogan, USA
3. Hayes Alan Jenkins, USA
1953 Davos
1. Hayes Alan Jenkins, USA
2. James D. Grogan, USA
3. Carlo Fassi, Italy
1954 Oslo
1. Hayes Alan Jenkins, USA
2. James D. Grogan, USA
3. Alain Giletti, France
1955 Vienna
1. Hayes Alan Jenkins, USA
2. Ronald Robertson, USA
3. David Jenkins, USA
1956 Garmisch-Partenkirchen
1. Hayes Alan Jenkins, USA
2. Ronald Robertson, USA
3. David Jenkins, USA
1957 Colorado Springs
1. David Jenkins, USA
2. Tim Brown, USA
3. Charles Snelling, Canada
1958 Paris
1. David Jenkins, USA
2. Tim Brown, USA
3. Alain Giletti, France
1959 Colorado Springs
1. David Jenkins, USA
2. Donald Jackson, Canada
3. Tim Brown, USA

(*b*) Women's Championships

1906 Davos
1. Madge Syers-Cave, Gt Britain
2. Jenny Herz, Austria

3. Lily Kronberger, Hungary
1907 Vienna
  1. Madge Syers-Cave, Gt Britain
  2. Jenny Herz, Austria
  3. Lily Kronberger, Hungary
1908 Troppau
  1. Lily Kronberger, Hungary
  2. Elsa Rendschmidt, Germany
1909 Budapest
  1. Lily Kronberger, Hungary
1910 Berlin
  1. Lily Kronberger, Hungary
  2. Elsa Rendschmidt, Germany
1911 Vienna
  1. Lily Kronberger, Hungary
  2. O.v. Méray Horváth, Hungary
  3. Ludowika Eilers, Germany
1912 Davos
  1. O.v. Méray Horváth, Hungary
  2. Grennhough Smith, Gt Britain
  3. Phyllis Johnson, Gt Britain
1913 Stockholm
  1. O.v. Méray Horváth, Hungary
  2. Phyllis Johnson, Gt Britain
  3. Svea Norén, Sweden
1914 St Moritz
  1. O.v. Méray Horváth, Hungary
  2. Angela Hanka, Austria
  3. Phyllis Johnson, Gt Britain
1915-1921 No competition
1922 Stockholm
  1. Herma Plank-Szabo, Austria
  2. Svea Norén, Sweden
  3. Margot Moe, Norway
1923 Vienna
  1. Herma Plank-Szabo, Austria

2. Gisela Reichmann, Austria
3. Svea Norén, Sweden
1924 Oslo
    1. Herma Plank-Szabo, Austria
    2. Ellen Brockhöfft, Germany
    3. Beatrix Loughran, USA
1925 Davos
    1. Herma Jaross-Szabo, Austria
    2. Ellen Brockhöfft, Germany
    3. Elisabeth Böckel, Germany
1926 Stockholm
    1. Herma Jaross-Szabo, Austria
    2. Sonja Henie, Norway
    3. Kathleen Shaw, Gt Britain
1927 Oslo
    1. Sonja Henie, Norway
    2. Herma Jaross-Szabo, Austria
    3. Karen Simensen, Norway
1928 London
    1. Sonja Henie, Norway
    2. Maribel Vinson, USA
    3. Fritzi Burger, Austria
1929 Budapest
    1. Sonja Henie, Norway
    2. Fritzi Burger, Austria
    3. Melitta Brunner, Austria
1930 New York
    1. Sonja Henie, Norway
    2. Cecil Eustace Smith, Canada
    3. Maribel Vinson, USA
1931 Berlin
    1. Sonja Henie, Norway
    2. Hilde Holovsky, Austria
    3. Fritzi Burger, Austria
1932 Montreal
    1. Sonja Henie, Norway

2. Fritzi Burger, Austria
3. Constance Wilson-Samuel, Canada

1933 Stockholm
1. Sonja Henie, Norway
2. Vivi-Anne Hultén, Sweden
3. Hilde Holovsky, Austria

1934 Oslo
1. Sonja Henie, Norway
2. Megan Taylor, Gt Britain
3. Liselotte Landbeck, Austria

1935 Vienna
1. Sonja Henie, Norway
2. Cecilia Colledge, Gt Britain
3. Vivi-Anne Hultén, Sweden

1936 Paris
1. Sonja Henie, Norway
2. Megan Taylor, Gt Britain
3. Vivi-Anne Hultén, Sweden

1937 London
1. Cecilia Colledge, Gt Britain
2. Megan Taylor, Gt Britain
3. Vivi-Anne Hultén, Sweden

1938 Stockholm
1. Megan Taylor, Gt Britain
2. Cecilia Colledge, Gt Britain
3. Hedy Stenuf, USA

1939 Prague
1. Megan Taylor, Gt Britain
2. Hedy Stenuf, USA
3. Daphne Walker, Gt Britain

1940-1946 No competition

1947 Stockholm
1. Barbara Ann Scott, Canada
2. Daphne Walker, Gt Britain
3. Gretchen Van Zandt Merrill, USA

1948 Davos
1. Barbara Ann Scott, Canada
2. Eva Pawlik, Austria
3. Jirina Nekolova, Czechoslovakia
1949 Paris
1. Alena Vrzanova, Czechoslovakia
2. Yvonne Sherman, USA
3. Jeannette Altwegg, Gt Britain
1950 London
1. Alena Vrzanova, Czechoslovakia
2. Jeannette Altwegg, Gt Britain
3. Yvonne Sherman, USA
1951 Milan
1. Jeannette Altwegg, Gt Britain
2. Jacqueline Du Bief, France
3. Sonja Klopfer, USA
1952 Paris
1. Jacqueline Du Bief, France
2. Sonja Klopfer, USA
3. Virginia Baxter, USA
1953 Davos
1. Tenley Albright, USA
2. Gundi Busch, Germany
3. Valda Osborn, Gt Britain
1954 Oslo
1. Gundi Busch, Germany
2. Tenley Albright, USA
3. Erica Batchelor, Gt Britain
1955 Vienna
1. Tenley Albright, USA
2. Carol Heiss, USA
3. Hanna Eigel, Austria
1956 Garmisch-Partenkirchen
1. Carol Heiss, USA
2. Tenley Albright, USA
3. Ingrid Wendl, Austria

1957 Colorado Springs
1. Carol Heiss, USA
2. Hanna Eigel, Austria
3. Ingrid Wendl, Austria
1958 Paris
1. Carol Heiss, USA
2. Ingrid Wendl, Austria
3. Hanna Walter, Austria
1959 Colorado Springs
1. Carol Heiss, USA
2. Hanna Walter, Austria
3. Sjoujke Dijkstra, Holland

(c) Pairs Championships

1908 St Petersburg (Leningrad)
1. Anna Hübler/Heinrich Burger, Germany
2. Phyllis and James Henry Johnson, Gt Britain
3. A. L. Fischer/L. P. Popowa, Russia
1909 Stockholm
1. Phyllis and James Henry Johnson, Gt Britain
2. Valborg Lindahl/Nils Rosenius, Sweden
3. Gertrud Ström/Richard Johanson, Sweden
1910 Berlin
1. Anna Hübler/Heinrich Burger, Germany
2. Ludowika Eilers/Walter Jakobsson, Germany/Finland
3. Phyllis and James Henry Johnson, Gt Britain
1911 Vienna
1. Ludowika Eilers/Walter Jakobsson, Germany/Finland
1912 Manchester
1. Phyllis and James Henry Johnson, Gt Britain
2. Ludowika and Walter Jakobsson-Eilers, Finland
3. Alexia and Ingvar Bryn-Schöyen, Norway
1913 Stockholm
1. Helene Engelmann/Karl Mejstrik, Austria
2. Ludowika and Walter Jakobsson-Eilers, Finland

3. Christa v. Szabo/Leo Horwitz, Austria
1914 St Moritz
1. Ludowika and Walter Jakobsson-Eilers, Finland
2. Helene Engelmann/Karl Mejstrik, Austria
3. Christa v. Szabo/Leo Horwitz, Austria
1915-1921 No competition
1922 Davos
1. Helene Engelmann/Alfred Berger, Austria
2. Ludowika and Walter Jakobsson-Eilers, Finland
3. Margarete and Paul Metzner, Germany
1923 Christiania (Oslo)
1. Ludowika and Walter Jakobsson-Eilers, Finland
2. Alexia and Ingvar Bryn-Schöyen, Norway
3. Elna Henrikson/Kaj af Edström, Sweden
1924 Manchester
1. Helene Engelmann/Alfred Berger, Austria
2. Ethel Muckelt/John F. Page, Gt Britain
3. Elna Henrikson/Kaj af Edström, Sweden
1925 Vienna
1. Herma Jaross-Szabo/Ludwig Wrede, Austria
2. Andrée Joly/Pierre Brunet, France
3. Lily Scholz/Otto Kaiser, Austria
1926 Berlin
1. Andrée Joly/Pierre Brunet, France
2. Lily Scholz/Otto Kaiser, Austria
3. Herma Jaross-Szabo/Ludwig Wrede, Austria
1927 Vienna
1. Herma Jaross-Szabo/Ludwig Wrede, Austria
2. Lily Scholz/Otto Kaiser, Austria
3. Lisl and Oskar Hoppe, Austria
1928 London
1. Andrée Joly/Pierre Brunet, France
2. Lily Scholz/Otto Kaiser, Austria
3. Melitta Brunner/Ludwig Wrede, Austria
1929 Budapest
1. Lily Scholz/Otto Kaiser, Austria

216

2. Melitta Brunner/Ludwig Wrede, Austria
3. Olga Organista/Alex. Szalay, Hungary
1930 New York
1. Andrée and Pierre Brunet-Joly, France
2. Melitta Brunner/Ludwig Wrede, Austria
3. Beatrix Loughran/Sherwin C. Badger, USA
1931 Berlin
1. Emilie Rotter/Laszlo Szollas, Hungary
2. Olga Organista/Szandor Szalay, Hungary
3. Idi Papez/Karl Zwack, Austria
1932 Montreal
1. Andrée and Pierre Brunet-Joly, France
2. Emilie Rotter/Laszlo Szollas, Hungary
3. Beatrix Loughran/Sherwin C. Badger, USA
1933 Stockholm
1. Emilie Rotter/Laszlo Szollas, Hungary
2. Idi Papez/Karl Zwack, Austria
3. Randi Bakke/Christen Christenson, Norway
1934 Helsingfors
1. Emilie Rotter/Laszlo Szollas, Hungary
2. Idi Papez/Karl Zwack, Austria
3. Maxi Herber/Ernst Baier, Germany
1935 Budapest
1. Emilie Rotter/Laszlo Szollas, Hungary
2. Ilse and Erik Pausin, Austria
3. Lucy Gallo/Reszoe Dillinger, Hungary
1936 Paris
1. Maxi Herber/Ernst Baier, Germany
2. Ilse and Erik Pausin, Austria
3. Violet and Leslie Cliff, Gt Britain
1937 London
1. Maxi Herber/Ernst Baier, Germany
2. Ilse and Erik Pausin, Austria
3. Violet and Leslie Cliff, Gt Britain
1938 Berlin
1. Maxi Herber/Ernst Baier, Germany

217

2. Ilse and Erik Pausin, Austria
3. Inge Koch/Günther Noack, Germany

1939 Budapest
1. Maxi Herber/Ernst Baier, Germany
2. Ilse and Erik Pausin, Austria
3. Inge Koch/Günther Noack, Germany

1940-1946 No competition

1947 Stockholm
1. Micheline Lannoy/Pierre Baugniet, Belgium
2. Karol and Peter Kennedy, USA
3. Suzanne Diskeuve/Edmond Verbustel, Belgium

1948 Davos
1. Micheline Lannoy/Pierre Baugniet, Belgium
2. Andrea Kékessy/Ede Király, Hungary
3. Suzanne Morrow/Wallace Diestelmeyer, Canada

1949 Paris
1. Andrea Kékessy/Ede Király, Hungary
2. Karol and Peter Kennedy, USA
3. Ann Davies/Carleton Hoffner, USA

1950 London
1. Karol and Peter Kennedy, USA
2. Jennifer and John Nicks, Gt Britain
3. Marianne and Laszlo Nagy, Hungary

1951 Milan
1. Ria Baran/Paul Falk, Germany
2. Karol and Peter Kennedy, USA
3. Jennifer and John Nicks, Gt Britain

1952 Paris
1. Ria and Paul Falk, Germany
2. Karol and Peter Kennedy, USA
3. Jennifer and John Nicks, Gt Britain

1953 Davos
1. Jennifer and John Nicks, Gt Britain
2. Francis Dafoe/Norris Bowden, Canada
3. Marianne and Laszlo Nagy, Hungary

1954 Oslo
1. Frances Dafoe/Norris Bowden, Canada
2. Sylvia and Michel Grandjean, Switzerland
3. Sissy Schwarz/Kurt Oppelt, Austria

1955 Vienna
1. Frances Dafoe/Norris Bowden, Canada
2. Sissy Schwarz/Kurt Oppelt, Austria
3. Marianne and Laszlo Nagy, Hungary

1956 Garmisch-Partenkirchen
1. Sissy Schwarz/Kurt Oppelt, Austria
2. Frances Dafoe/Norris Bowden, Canada
3. Marika Kilius/Franz Ningel, Germany

1957 Colorado Springs
1. Barbara Wagner/Robert Paul, Canada
2. Marika Kilius/Franz Ningel, Germany
3. Maria and Otto Jelinek, Canada

1958 Paris
1. Barbara Wagner/Robert Paul, Canada
2. Vera Suchanková/Zdenek Dolezal, Czechoslovakia
3. Maria and Otto Jelinek, Canada

1959 Colorado Springs
1. Barbara Wagner/Robert Paul, Canada
2. Marika Kilius/Hans-Jürgen Bäumler, Western Germany
3. Nancy and Ronald Ludington, USA

(*d*) Ice-dancing Championships

1952 Paris
1. Jean Westwood/Lawrence Demmy, Gt Britain
2. Joan Dewhirst/John Slater, Gt Britain
3. Carol Peters/Daniel Ryan, USA

1953 Davos
1. Jean Westwood/Lawrence Demmy, Gt Britain
2. Joan Dewhirst/John Slater, Gt Britain
3. Carol Peters/Daniel Ryan, USA

1954 Oslo
1. Jean Westwood/Lawrence Demmy, Gt Britain
2. Nesta Davies/Paul Thomas, Gt Britain
3. Carol and Edward Bodel, USA

1955 Vienna
1. Jean Westwood/Lawrence Demmy, Gt Britain
2. Pamela Weight/Paul Thomas, Gt Britain
3. Barbara Radford/Raymond Lockwood, Gt Britain

1956 Garmisch-Partenkirchen
1. Pamela Weight/Paul Thomas, Gt Britain
2. June Markham/Courtney Jones, Gt Britain
3. Barbara Thompson/Gerald Rigby, Gt Britain

1957 Colorado Springs
1. June Markham/Courtney Jones, Gt Britain
2. Geraldine Fenton/W. McLachlan, Canada
3. Sharon McKenzie/Bert Wright, USA

1958 Paris
1. June Markham/Courtney Jones, Gt Britain
2. Geraldine Fenton/W. McLachlan, Canada
3. Andrée Anderson/Donald Jacoby, USA

1959 Colorado Springs
1. Doreen Denny/Courtney Jones, Gt Britain
2. Andrée and Donald Jacoby, USA
3. Geraldine Fenton/William MacLaughlin, Canada